THE
BEST
BRITISH
POETRY

2011

◇   ◇   ◇

RODDY LUMSDEN (born 1966) is a Scottish poet, who was born in St Andrews. He has published six collections of poetry, a number of chapbooks and a collection of trivia, as well as editing a generational anthology of British and Irish poets of the 1990s and 2000s, *Identity Parade*. He lives in London where he teaches for The Poetry School. He has done editing work on several prize-winning poetry collections and edited the Pilot series of chapbooks by poets under 30 for tall-lighthouse. He is organiser and host of the monthly reading series BroadCast in London. In 2010, he was appointed as Poetry Editor for Salt Publishing.

THE
BEST
BRITISH
POETRY

2011

RODDY LUMSDEN, *Series Editor*

SALT

LONDON

PUBLISHED BY SALT PUBLISHING
Acre House, 11-15 William Road, London NW1 3ER United Kingdom

Selection and introduction © Roddy Lumsden, 2011
Individual contributions © the contributors

Printed in Great Britain by Clays Ltd, St Ives plc

Typeset in Bembo 10.5 / 12

ISBN 978 1 90773 04 4 paperback

1 3 5 7 9 8 6 4 2

CONTENTS

Introduction by Roddy Lumsden   ix

Gillian Allnutt, "in her kitchen"   1
Mike Bannister, "Satin Moth"   2
Chris Beckett, "Boast of the Fly-Whisk"   3
Emily Berry, "Sweet Arlene"   5
Liz Berry, "The Year We Married Birds"   7
Nina Boyd, "Lanterns"   9
James Brookes, "Opiates: Kaliningrad"   10
Judy Brown, "The Helicopter Visions"   11
Mark Burnhope, "Twelve Steps Towards Better Despair"   13
Kayo Chingonyi, "Andrew's Corner"   15
Jane Commane, "Music"   17
Fred D'Aguiar, "The Rose of Toulouse"   18
Emma Danes, "17"   21
Amy De'Ath, "Lena at the Beach"   22
Isobel Dixon, "A Beautifully Constructed Cocktail"   25
Sasha Dugdale, "Shepherds"   27
Ian Duhig, "Jericho Shandy"   29
Josh Ekroy, "78 rpm"   32
Laura Elliott, "White Lace Nightgown"   33
Carrie Etter, "Prairie"   34
Dai George, "Poolside at Le Domaine"   35
Giles Goodland, "Waves"   36
Matthew Gregory, "Young Pterodactyl"   38
Philip Gross, "Later"   40
Kelly Grovier, "A Butterfly in the British Museum"   42
Jen Hadfield, "The Ambition"   43
Aiko Harman, "Hitodama (人魂 or 'Human Soul')"   45
Emily Hasler, "Valediction"   46
Oli Hazzard, "Sonnet"   47
W.N. Herbert, from "Errant"   48
Alexander Hutchison, "Deil Tak The Hinmaist"   51
Sarah Jackson, "Light Over Ratcliffe"   53
Christopher James, "The Retired Eunuch"   54
Katharine Kilalea, "Hennecker's Ditch"   55
Nick Laird, "Collusion"   60
Pippa Little, "Coal End Hill Farm 1962"   61

Chris McCabe, "Kingfisher"   62
Ted McCarthy, "Beverly Downs"   64
John McCullough, "Sleeping Hermaphrodite"   65
Patrick McGuinness, "House Clearance"   66
Kona Macphee, "My Life as a B Movie"   67
Lorraine Mariner, "And then there will be no more nonsense"   69
Sophie Mayer, "Of Other Spaces (Tate St. Ives)"   70
Gordon Meade, "Rats"   71
Matt Merritt, "Pluvialis"   72
Kate Miller, "The Apple Farmers' Calendar"   74
Esther Morgan, "Short-hold"   75
Catherine Ormell, "Delicacy"   76
Richard Osmond, "Logo"   77
Ruth Padel, "Only Here On Earth"   78
Emma Page, "California"   79
Nii Ayikwei Parkes, "Lapse"   80
Abigail Parry, "Hare"   81
Andrew Philip, "10 × 10"   83
Heather Phillipson, "At First, the Only Concern is Milk,   87
    More or Less"
Kate Potts, "Three Wishes"   88
Vidyan Ravinthiran, "Anti-circ"   89
Deryn Rees-Jones, from "The Songs of Elisabeth So"   90
Sam Riviere, "Honeymoon"   94
Colette Sensier, "Orpheus"   95
Penelope Shuttle, "The Year Strikes the Rock"   98
Jon Stone, "Mustard"   100
Matthew Sweeney, "Communiqué"   101
George Szirtes, "Some Sayings about the Snake"   102
Lizzi Thistlethwayte, "Scart Gap"   103
Eoghan Walls, "The Long Horizon"   104
Ahren Warner, "Hasard"   106
Chrissy Williams, "Sheep"   108
Samantha Wynne-Rhydderch, "Table Manners"   110
Michael Zand, "on a persian cairn"   111

Contributors' Notes and Comments   115
List of Magazines   157
Acknowledgements   161

INTRODUCTION

by Roddy Lumsden

◊   ◊   ◊

The poems presented in this volume were selected from UK-based poetry magazines, literary journals and online publications issued between spring 2010 and spring 2011. The main purpose of this volume is to celebrate the thriving scene of literary magazines and the developing sphere of literary sites online. For the past year, I have been reading these publications as they appeared, seeking poems which struck me as enjoyable, rewarding, accomplished . . . I could continue with such adjectives but, in the end, I was not looking for poems to tick boxes; I merely read, with a mix of personal taste and an attempt at a consensus of opinion, and selected the pieces which brought an instinctive 'yes' when I reached the poem's end.

The format of the book owes a debt to *The Best American Poetry* series of anthologies which was founded in 1988. Similar volumes appear each year in Canada, Australia and Ireland. We have not previously had such a book in the UK, partly because of the existence of a similar series, *The Forward Book of Poetry*, which has been appearing annually since the early 1990s to coincide with National Poetry Day and the Forward Prizes. The Forward series does a good job, but its main aim is to select from published books and only a handful of poems from magazines now appear each year. At a time when print publications are threatened by funding problems and the recession, and when online publications are becoming more common and more attractive, it seems right to gather some of the best work from these sources, to showcase the strength and breadth of what is appearing there.

Now let's deal with the B word. We have decided to go with the familiar branding in other countries of such books as 'Best X Poetry'. All of these books, at some time, have been questioned on the use of the debatable word 'best'. What best? Whose best? The word irks some people who feel that the subjective nature of selecting and editing a book like this is at odds with such an objective word as 'best'. I can see that, but there is no manifesto behind the word, no ulterior motive. If it really bothers anyone, a cup of tea and a nap might help. These were the poems I felt were best, of all the poems I read. Someone else would have made a different selection, and next year, another editor will do so, as I retreat into my capacity as Series Editor, leaving much of the decision making to my guest editor who, in 2012, will be the Carcanet/Oxford poet Sasha Dugdale.

The gathering of work involved was hugely helped by the resources of The Saison Poetry Library, housed in the Southbank Centre in London. I went there every few weeks during the reading period and gathered a pile of the latest magazines from the racks, making photocopies of any poems I felt were likely candidates. The Library stocks the latest editions of all publications it is aware of, ranging from small zines to long-standing literary journals. I also made use of their list of online publications. The end result is, I hope, a snapshot of what is happening at present in non-book publication of poetry in the UK, with poems selected from long-established literary journals such as *Poetry Review*, *Agenda* and *PN Review* alongside small magazines such as *Rising*, *South Bank Poetry* and *Obsessed With Pipework* and online sites such as *QUID*, *Shadowtrain* and *Ink Sweat and Tears*.

A few things eluded me — one poem I wished to include turned out to be reprinted from a volume from many years ago, another was by a poet who was on an extended trip and uncontactable. It interests me to note that the 70 poems included split exactly 50/50 gender-wise, something I had not been keeping note of. There is an interesting mix of well-known names, less-known ones and emerging poets. At a time when the average age of published poets is steadily climbing, I'm pleased to note that around a quarter of the poets here are under 30, representing a coming generation which I believe to be the strongest ever in UK poetry (and a reflection of the fact that young poets continue to engage with the magazine scene, perhaps more than older or more established poets).

Readers may be surprised to find no poems from the two main UK literary newspapers, the *TLS* and *London Review of Books*. The former continues to publish a welcome amount of poems in most issues but none of them caught my eye, while the latter seems to favour non-UK poets on the whole. A number of publications deserve a mention for their efforts, not least *Poetry London* which published more poems presented here than any other publication. Under the editorship of Colette Bryce, *Poetry London* has flourished, with a variety and quality unmatched by any other publication representing mainstream poetry. *New Welsh Review*, under Kathryn Gray and now Gwen Davies, is another journal which is flourishing. *Gutter*, a new magazine from Scotland, is attracting work from the finest poets north of the border. Another rich resource for me was *The Rialto* which had given space over a few issues to Nathan Hamilton to solicit work by a younger generation of UK poets.

The poets included here are either from the UK or are based here — there are poets originally from the US, South Africa, Ghana, Ireland, Iran and elsewhere. They also come from the various constituencies of poetry, mainstream and non-mainstream, lyric, formal and experimental. There are more than four decades in age between the oldest and youngest. There are poets here who are long acclaimed with many collections published, alongside relative newcomers (one poet, Emma Page, is represented by her first published poem). More than a third of the poets are yet to publish a collection. The book shows a varied and thriving UK poetry scene played out across a multitude of magazines and websites, many of them provided by people working for little or no money.

THE
BEST
BRITISH
POETRY
2011

◇   ◇   ◇

GILLIAN ALLNUTT

in her kitchen

◇　◇　◇

delphinium

the heart, fleet, in its large domain

a *grand meaulnes*

summer, recalled, a light blue lent sea

of dust and shadow, now, the house

of doubtfulness

who, in the hospital, implored them—

deep in daylight, implicate, a crowd

hours pass, unrecalled

the heart, a striped tent in a field

from *Poetry Review*

MIKE BANNISTER

Satin Moth

◊ ◊ ◊

(Leucoma Salicis — Lymantriidae)

Silence for the ghost of silence;
in pitch dark, I find a white-winged moth
at rest where I was sleeping just a while ago;
her wings, where mine would be; soft brilliance,
perfect moon on a quiet river, spotless lint,
traced with veins of mistletoe.

Defiant *Lymantriide*, you advertise,
against the protocols of subterfuge,
flaring, pristine, rebellious in the night;
stealing in to our dream on soundless wings
to taste the obscure chemistries we share
with poplars, or the willow leaf.

I cup her out into the warm night,
then lie awake, considering the metaphoric
significance of ordinary things; the hundred
thousandth possibility of meaning: the Zen
of white, of black, of the night messenger:
stillness for the ghost of stillness.

from *Other Poetry*

CHRIS BECKETT

Boast of the Fly-Whisk

◇ ◇ ◇

Tail without a horse! hair of the horse called
    Smoke-with-a-Tail
fierce flayer of wasps and fleas

I salute you, Gashay! relaxing on this cushy knee
    in sunny slug-warm garden

but here come
two fat scuttle flies
with feet
for sick and stink

Master! who wears his hang-dog like a shirt
don't throw me down
and let the hairy bandits suck your tongue

    life is meaningless, you wail,
      let them feast on me!

do not believe the mild voice of whisk

    such a soft name!

my black rope handle is unforgiving
my rough chopping mane is cut in the shape of a torch

I am the thing from your past that you must hold on to
    at all costs
your thin flowing backbone of proud and tough
I am your old-man boy

tell me, who killed the loutish hornet when you were six?

who shattered the pack of parsley wasps and carrot flies?

shall I not assist you now that your whole construction of clean and
    light
   is at risk?

Master! I yellow at my fringe but still I am lighter
   than a kalash
my grisly hair is itching for a fight

from *Smiths Knoll*

Gashay: respectful name for an older man, literally "my shield" (Amharic)
Kalash: short for Kalashnikov

Sweet Arlene

◇   ◇   ◇

In Arlene's house we live above the mutilated floor.
Arlene tells us: This is what you do. This is what you don't.
We keep watch over the reddening ivy. We take off our shoes
indoors and don't hang up our coats and never mind
the cold and the bleak outlook. We think of other moments.
Baby, baby, baby. Take me home. Arlene has us in one room.
At night we smother the window with a system of blankets
and a towel balanced on the end of a broom. We remain sane
despite the worrisome nature of details. All day we are smuggled
through a city where ivy rests against walls seeming incredibly
peaceful and we wish it could teach us something. We say,
Thank you, Arlene. Thanks for this opportunity. Thanks
for this shaft of light lying like a plank across the floor.
Thanks for the visceral scrape of the freezer trays,
and for a picture of a lady with no clothes on. Most of all,
thank you, Arlene, for giving us things we did not have before,
like the chance to eat pears while looking out the window
at a pear tree. We've confessed to Arlene: knees to our chests
in the usual position, we repeated our ritual of shiver, breathe.
We recited our mantras but they came out crooked and strange.
We wished we had faith. We made this prayer, a faithless one,
it took all our energy to say: Please help. We kneeled up in bed,
we had the sheets in our hands like ropes. We needed something
to hold. We sent it out. We didn't know if we talking to God,
or Arlene, or someone else. She was behind us like a devil.
The devil had her hand on my back and she stroked our hair
and she was Sweet Arlene. We clung to Sweet Arlene and to
Arlene's whisper. It was peace of some kind. But we couldn't
trust her. We were scared and we'd been up all night.
Sorry, Arlene. Our prayer was too weak. We were too tired
to repeat our spell. On the tape a doctor's voice said:
Imagine a place. We did and that place was Arlene's house.

All the colourful knobs of the oven and the rickety pans and Arlene
in the quiet being wickedly calm. I called my baby. Take me home.
I said: We're afraid of Arlene's house and we're not safe in our bones.
We rattled and kept ourselves awake. We knocked and knocked.
Arlene gathered us up. She cradled us and shook us till we made
a sound like a rain stick and we tried to materialise: I tried to be
cheeks and hips and everything you need in a woman. We woke
on a plane and my head was on my baby's lap and I thought Arlene
had left us. When we landed my spirit was a rose, we boarded a train
and I understood everything, I felt akin to the gleaming haunches
of the taxi. Arlene did not. We shushed her and rocked her,
just like she taught us. We carried her back to our house.

from *Poetry London*

The Year We Married Birds

◇   ◇   ◇

That year, with men turning thirty
still refusing to fly the nest,
we married birds instead.

Migrating snow buntings
swept into offices in the city,
took flocks of girls for Highland weddings.

Magpies smashed jewellers' windows,
kites hovered above bridal shops,
a pigeon in Trafalgar Square learnt to kneel.

Sales of nesting boxes soared.
Soon cinemas were wild as woods in May
while restaurants served worms.

By June, a Russian kittiwake wed
the Minister's daughter, gave her two
freckled eggs, a mansion on a cliff.

My own groom was a kingfisher:
enigmatic, bright. He gleamed in a metallic
turquoise suit, taught me about fishing

in the murky canal. We honeymooned
near the Wash, the saltmarshes
booming with courting bittern.

When I think of that year, I remember best
the fanning of his feathers
on my cheek, his white throat,

how every building, every street rang
with birdsong. How girls' wedding dresses
lifted them into the trees like wings.

from *Brittle Star*

NINA BOYD

Lanterns

◇　◇　◇

In the paddock where we saw you last
a foal with trestle table legs leans
into its mother's flank.
Wind fans the grass.

I have watched you stroke the back
of a bumble bee, your finger lenient
as the violet tongue that flicks
a staggering calf.

We haven't seen you since
a drift of lanterns sailed above our heads,
gaudy orange thumbprints
on a mares' tail sky.

You climbed into that night,
waving your hat; leaving behind
the breath of cattle,
earth-bound tethered beasts.

from *Iota*

Opiates: Kaliningrad

◇　◇　◇

Scilicet the bar at the back of the restaurant:
ampoules of creosote, methadone, spermaceti.

You have in your possession
the medal for the capture of Königsburg:

a brimstone of cupro-nickel, saffron of tarnish.
Agreed. You may have passage

to the lost Amber Room. Where fire
burnished the quarters, the Löbenicht and Kneiphof,

to a shell case brass, there's now a nuclear
installation; a cartel of tonic peddlers.

By knocking off time, the sun is in suspension,
joyless at its weight as alloyed gold.

from *The Wolf*

JUDY BROWN

The Helicopter Visions

◊ ◊ ◊

You'd never believe how easy it is
to lose your way—how our bearings slur
as we cross the city in under ten minutes,
tracing the parks where London splits to green.
How the dawn breaks open, orange and fatal,
like a pomegranate landing on concrete.

Or how our instruments see too much
perhaps—from the itch of the chestnut candles
starting to fire to tigerworms threading
the compost heaps with red. And down there:
that pair of pale trousers prone on the decking,
rained-on and stained with chianti.

But I've come to crave exactly this—
the taste of the morning before it's tainted;
I'm the man who watches rush-hour build
like silver coral. I crack the codes—the dots
and checks on squad cars—or shadow
the mercy dash of an ambulance.

All too soon we hang overhead, a thudding
barge of air, settle our weight into the slack,
the landing space. Even now it shakes me
when the crowded colours of earth stripe the glass
as we're suddenly sucked down. We spill—
friction hot—into the morning at Willesden.

The ground seems to bruise my feet
as I head for my cooling bed, where only
a just-warm dent remains of a dayshift girlfriend.
And above me the gods are strung
like fine chandeliers and I admit to myself
without surprise: *I do not want to be home.*

from *Ambit*

Twelve Steps Towards Better Despair

◇   ◇   ◇

Rehearse its salt between your fingers often, vigorously.

Have it amalgamate into your petrol-slick tinted lethargy.

Write of the cormorant's yellow beak over her black body.

The iceberg: for a sound few seconds, it will stand
for solid material to marvel at. It need not sink your battleship
before you shy away from it. So don't bemoan its tip, thank it.

Make sure you have shouldered the world for a man who tried
dying—sorry, *died trying*—to climb a cliff summit,
or summat like it, to find a stronger sunlight.

Write of the good in global warming, icebergs melting, salt.

Recite names of the dead on your fingers often, vigorously.

Have their ashes sown into the stinking spumes of elegy.

Write of the widow's blonde wig over her black bodice.

Go fearlessly: for a modest seventy years we'll stand,
most of us men, to be gawped at; never forget that. So choose
your battles, and—if you buy—the best cruiser in the marina.

Make sure you have shouldered rope for a man who tied
skilfully: docked a boat and helped his lover onto the land
for both to stand under the cliffs and observe a cormorant.

Find and write of the good in swiftly dying—sorry, *flying*.

from *Magma*

Andrew's Corner

◇ ◇ ◇

I

Where an old man comes, to practice
standing still, tutting
that the street he fought to keep is gone
and, sixty years on, he doesn't belong
to this world of bass, blasting out of
passing cars, and earshot, at the speed
of an age when pubs close down
overnight; are mounds of rubble in a week.

II

Where flowers moulder in memory of Tash,
fifteen, her twenty-something boyfriend
too drunk to swerve and miss the tree,
girls own their grown woman outfits,
smile at boys who smell of weed and too much
CK One. Pel, who can get served, stands in line.
Outside his friends play the transatlantic
dozens; the correct answer is always your mum.

III

Where alleys wake to condom wrappers,
kebab meat, a ballet pump, last week
a van pulled up and it was blood. Today:
joggers dodge a dead pigeon, offer wordless
greeting to the night bus's army of sanguine-

eyed ravers, nursing bad skin and tinnitus.
Goaded by the light, past the same house on repeat,
they think of taking off their shoes; inviolable sleep.

from *Wasafiri*

Music

◊ ◊ ◊

In the monotone riot of another dead composer
we have chosen to write an anthem for the school.

It will be composed of skiving off and *Suicide Alley*,
the sound of civic pigeons colonising the silverware,

the clash of boy-meets-girl-meets-tragic-ensemble-of-light
somewhere beyond the silos of a different town just like this.

It will be composed of all the kids left on the offside
when the time comes to pick the year's team of winners

and the distilled anger of the never-heard singer-songwriter's
broken gamut of strings, detuned to a finer chord of O.

Written on toilet walls, it will exist for three days,
four nights, before the janitorial chorus swash of bleach
makes better of the notes.

from *Tears in the Fence*

The Rose of Toulouse

◇ ◇ ◇

I

If it exists, smells of buttered croissants,
Strawberry jam and *café au lait*.

The anti-terrorist knife just about splits
Crumbly, boomerang-shaped bread and sends
Legions marching to Paris in Roman formation

Patterns of the dominated, with a streetwise hip
And nightclub hop and not a slave to be seen,
And certainly not a scene for former slaves

Or their feisty descendants, wearing their life
Savings, nursing wounds from history, no track
Record in an ocean with bones for a library.

2

This is my last morning in this town,
But not the last town I will see this morning.

I head for the capital where the talk
Is less sonorous as sonorous goes,
And more clipped, for clipped is as clipped does,

With the colonial emblems of slaves on the streets
Looking proprietorial in their Nike fatigues,
My brothers and sisters in arms, in the daily

Grind to keep that grin and in-your-face,
Game-face from turning sour, keep dancing
For suppers and lucky strikes.

3

I love this time to myself and miss my kids
Climbing all over my writing routine pretence,

When I want nothing to do with them
And want nothing to do with anything
That does not include them in it.

My dreams do not count, too many to count,
I recount the majority as nightmares.
Please do not give me what I ask for.

I do not know what I want;
I do not want what I know.
I am in at least two minds about this,

4

That and *de tarat* as Guyanese say
Waving away confusion morphed into

Pesky houseflies craving salt on a brow.
There is a word for my condition,
But I won't find it and cure myself.

There is a condition for my words
Spread slap-dash method on a palette
Governed by mood, governed, in turn,

By shape-shift focus as if that imagined
Rose of Toulouse with a city mix of sweets,
Grime and sirens, could ever be real.

For this shared bread, for the multitudes
Housed in cardboard shelters on artificial hills

Of a city's fuming rubbish, and for my children
Whose gleeful faces rise in bubbles containing
Sky and everything underneath, as they sail

From me seeking death's light touch,
More a soundless kiss of dissolution
Of earth, sky and everything in between, I say,

We were people before we were slaves, pirates,
Or prostitutes with looks and matching smell,
And this come on, 'sport me in your lapel.'

from *Poetry London*

17

◊　◊　◊

We thought it would be ours—shy-on
to the street, inadequate fence,
blind corners. We learned it by night—
its Braille of angles and doorways,
its patois of rattle and crack.

We dismantled the chimney stack,
offered up wiring and roof slates,
carpentry. We brought it a child.
It bristled with splinters and snagged
nails. We practised to be smaller.

It longed to be empty, tethered
behind the bus stop in the shade
of a constancy of trees. One
dawn we slipped out between the teeth
of the lock we'd fitted, arrived

where even cow parsley's lighter—
a child's hands feathered with flour.
Postmen and plumbers attend us.
In the park, no widowed swan guards
the bruise of her reflection.

from *Poetry News*

Lena at the Beach

◇ ◇ ◇

In the blossom of the brain, in so far as I am people,
in terms of my churlishness in the context of a lowering
sky of lifestyle, being a person moreover, being a person
takeover, in identifying people it helps to consider a
person a salty brick, the lusty exposition left of a person
leftover alongside sheepish person subjects in any
rearticulation of a person the people are on dodgy
ground, in misreading the script of being beauty I was
black beauty and a womaniser.

Who cares about the psychosocial fabrications of a lusty brick?

What if it's wrong?

What if I want to lie, compete, ease my conscience on a salty brick?

Rest my hot cheek pearling beads of salt onto the
perverse orange brick of saturated consolation with
radical implications for all girls and boys who dare to be
churlish, who forget the brick and blossom of my body
and remember to speak through the irony of
windbreakers broken by the wind and tossed to sea in
the bedroom where no one has sex.

In the paranoid Huguenot daughter, in our margins we
love to be lofty, in my heart-thumping under scudding
clouds in my stomach when I think about it, in grouchy
thickets and bark's little teeth I'm again a Swedish
model looking over my shoulder at November 1972.

Arriving at the beach in the context of a coveting
style of life, in the scrubby bench I found again
my teeth,

I bit to chew and chewed hard to make it known
that I am not here for smiling, coyness, shyness, or was
it something I had in mind grinning growling yakking
making my presence felt or manning up, I was too
young for algorithms,

to be spewing myself out of windows off bridges in front of tube trains,
did I never want to learn poetry brick, no no!
I wanted only to write programs and lie down bucolic.

I lay in the sand and the dead moved over me, his long hair
lapped my leg and my oily sun cream and my Katrina,
my Santa Ana, I learned your names less subject-to-error
you move rapidly northward less I lose you all.

Give me your name.
Roll me down through a name's universal blue river
and give me.
Your name was not a gift but a given.

Donated Anita of stainless steel and Tetra Pack,
there is more truth in you, Anita of kulturlos I applause your cunning.

At the historical moment of your inception you were coming.

At the unconscious hill of habit.

In the comfort of the taking, to the extent the dead
men. However they died to me. However they sold
their wares on the doorstep on red tiles I saw them

through frosted glass I felt their hot panacean feet.
However I was born.

What penalty might be incurred
for succumbing?
Categorical uselessness
or my bucket of sand.

I grew boldly in their raunchy village, and wept frequently.

I rode home on several bicycles, I was ridden of doubt.

My little empire glowered.

from *QUID*

A Beautifully Constructed Cocktail

◇　◇　◇

Your beautifully constructed cocktails
became legendary
and you named them well,
a way of slipping poetry
into the bloodstream of the girls

too subtle for the Screaming Orgasm,
Sex on the Beach,
but glad to reach for every chilled
or minted, salted glass
you'd shake up, pour and pass

across the artful books
with the perfect sweet spot quip
or quote, the measured look,
depending on the lightness of the hour.
The Metamorphosis, Lure of the Sea,

The Rings of Saturn and the Abilene.
Cloud Atlas, The Trieste,
Sweet Beatrice, La Belle Confidente,
the Kandahar. These I recall
and more. Their cherry lips,

how you gauged them, like a Gideon,
on their gulps, or careful sips,
how long it took them not to care
about the glass-stem's snapping,
spilling syrup on the tablecloth,
about the liquid's naming, or their own.

from *Magma*

Shepherds

◊   ◊   ◊

Late June the ghosts of shepherds meet on the hills
And one has his crook with its musket barrel hook
One carries a Bible, and all wear the smock
And listen out for the little bells and the canister bells
Worn by the sheep and the big cattle, carried by the wind
Which shapes the hawthorn into mermaid's hair and open book.

There are those who died on the hills, and those who died in their beds,
The haloed, who wear a flame about them, were
Asleep in their wagons, the stove door ajar
The oil lamp tipped. And scores stamp
A last ghastly dawn patrol—their crook a rifle
Cigarettes for their bible.

The hills are not high. High enough
To exist outside us, our low troubles
At the school gates the children look up
And see with a shock of memory
That the earth gathers itself
Into another world
One closer to the sky

Once peopled by shepherds,
Who inherited the high roads from kings and saints
As they passed, withy ropes about their shoulders.
Who spoke little, and wore tall hats
Bawled gently at their dogs,
Who were themselves
Creatures apart

Times when the mist comes up
And rolls like weighted grey

Down the scarp, up there
The cars see their lamps reflected back
A metre ahead, and the back of her is silent
But never like a moor, never fierce like that
She'd carry you back to your own gate
On the palm of her hand—not bury you alive.

Her spine is a landshed, and a land of itself
A land of haunches and shoulders, and glistening fields
Impossible that they weren't in love with her
The kindness of her miles, the smalls of her back,
The blazing white of her summers.

The Bible is her book: she wrote it for her shepherds
To train them in oblivion and seasons
And the time she knows, the slowest time on earth
She wrote it in chalk, in rabbit droppings, and lady's smock
She wrote it in sweet marjoram and she adorned it with bells
And it has no meaning for anyone, except the shepherds
Who are gone.

from *Agenda*

IAN DUHIG

Jericho Shandy

◇   ◇   ◇

The surrealist machine is more often than not a nonfunctional machine
—SARA DARIUS, 'The Senses of Modernism'

Returning from the anniversary
event for Sterne at Bradford Library,
a theft of signal wire maroons his train
beside the Kirkstall Abbey points for Leeds,
a name which sounds a pun, but not to him.
He's feeling hemmed-in by the open space,
a paradoxophobia mixed with . . .
he wonders what word would mean 'fear of nature'—
gaiaphobia? or start with 'pan-',
as in panic, as in panic attack?
He notes Cornell alarm chains under glass,
a hammer under glass for breaking glass.
This Bradford route's a sideline to a sideline,
sidelined now, reflecting on itself,
he thinks, a black-silk-hatted parody,
a *Soft Cell* synth man who only plays
recessionals on his harmonium
as doors close on the coffin and the flames.
He checks the carriage doors. They're locked, of course.
He notes the engine idles in iambics,
growing more insistent all the time.
Distraction from distraction's what he needs;
he thinks of Henry 'Box' Brown, escaped slave,
who recreated on this line his flight
to Northern freedom from Virginia,
and then of Earnshaw, the unescaped artist,
boxmaker, anarchist, who rode here
on his famed Surrealist Expeditions,
now travelling just as fast, although he's dead,
as this steel coffin with an Abbey view.

There's no-one's in his carriage. Or the next,
bar one slumped goth, a daywalker in shades.
He sees the guard is smoking down the track.
Reminded of that traveller's tale from Twain
with mummies fuelling Egyptian trains,
he opens all the carriage windows wide
then gets a head of steam up for himself.
The flesh is grass that fuels his Proto Pipe,
distraction engine of the connoisseur;
a locomotive run on loco weed,
but pocket-sized, its firebox solid brass
with built-in poker, tar-trap, sliding smoke-cap—
Ceci n'est pas une pipe, but art to him
from stem to Sternesque incurled spinning smoke
that rhymes with wire abandoned by the thieves
to kink and bite its tail and arabesque
like drawings of Trim's gestures with his stick.
He draws until his head begins to spin,
thinks Northern Lights a good name for this grass . . .
When straight, he'd kill time on another line
by taking phone cold callers for a ride;
A timeshare? Great! But let's consider time!
He'd fugue on monastery prayer-routines
and Mumford's view their strictness gave the West
its grounding in machine-age discipline,
or Mrs Shandy winding up her husband;
Marx on clockless works; Toussaint L'Ouverture,
his gold watch stolen, exiled in the Jura,
where, in good time, the local watchmakers
would teach Kropotkin real-life anarchism . . .
None laughed, their English often second-hand,
commission making up their sweatshop pay,
his bourgeois deviationism stale,
reduced as one of Bennett's Talking Heads.
But now he listens with intensity
to sounds a swift makes harvesting the sky,
worms churning willowherb and meadowsweet,
the bull chained by its nose to a cartwheel,
a punky sun turning its wooden dial . . .
A tyre's soft watch drips slowly on a tree;
inside, paranoia's less critical
than *tumultuosissimamente*:
he's sure he's suffering Karmic punishment

for keeping hands from working in real life,
his Chinese watch, where copper scrap winds up,
the Golden Virginia in all those joints . . .
The robot heartbeat of the engine turns
to footsteps at his back, death in high heels,
while Kirkstall Abbey melts to Auden's face:
Stop all the clocks, cut off the telephone,
it says to Alan Bennett, *Poetry?*
But that's found far from outskirts such as these!
Remembering that Bennett lived near Troy,
by Horsforth Station, he thinks of Irwin,
Hector's foe, who lives there in the screenplay
though *Somewhere on the outskirts* on the stage;
then Bennett quoting Eliot on walls;
the History Boys against the National wall
on the book cover Darren Wall designed . . .
Convinced he's trapped now for eternity,
he thinks this page's walls are closing in,
then closes his own eyes to find himself
in his personal page 73:
he dreams evolved new fish will one day find
his cage of bones in the train's rusted cage
with Northern Lights' seeds growing through his ribs
a post-historic forest coast to coast,
his Proto Pipe all protozoic slime . . .
He shudders, then forgets why, at what.
He wonders if the goth brought chocolate.

from *Poetry Review*

78 rpm

◇ ◇ ◇

Oh Mein Papa, foxtrots,
none of them measured up.
The vibrato of an irate joker, trebles
slipping through the fog of static,
an oboe quarrelling with hiss.
They were trying too hard to please.
Didn't change the needle, you could
play it with a thorn. The tiny tin box
of used pinpricks was a waste of space.
Winding down, an old man sobbed,
bogged in mud, hilariously
lockjawed. This was more like it.

They broke easily but the label
held the sharp-edged pieces. Shellac:
a dog nosing an ear-trumpet
revved to a dizzying soup. The arm,
lowered, was a bird pecking
on the warp of a glistening wave of oil.
Scratched, the regular click confirmed me,
and when it faded. I'd frisbee them
like clay pigeons, but had no gun
to shatter them over waste ground.
The Vienna Boys' Choir was stung
into silence in the nettle patch.

from *Equinox*

White Lace Nightgown

◊   ◊   ◊

The sky blanches.
In the lemon half-sleep
my nipples are ring pulls.
I am clam-lipped.

The coffee mug in your palm
is a baby's crown,
violetwhite soap noses
suck the porcelain washbowl.

You plump my sunflowers;
insidious, pip-cyed,
they shiver.

from *Iota*

Prairie

◊ ◊ ◊

sprawling through night   a train's low horn
the crossings   empty   the ritual
maintained   reflex or   especial precaution

do the sleepers hear it   do their ears
make unconscious record   to litanize

prescience loses particularity   unbound
on prairie   to vague expectation
with or without   hope

with or without   the train whistle's
thread   reminder redeemer

of silence   each isolate mind
banked in prescience   if it's not nostalgia
impalpable   in small hours   impalpable

in the drift   as names ease from objects
unmannered ritual   especial   withoutness

from *Shearsman*

DAI GEORGE

Poolside at Le Domaine

◊   ◊   ◊

Brochures would dub those shutters *cornflower blue*
but me, I see a baron plunging out of them, the colour of his blood
pooling on the patio.

You've nipped inside to fix a drink or sleep
while somewhere close a mower chunters through the noon. Bushes slur
with insects. But I keep the peace,

reclining on a lounger semi-nude
within the *piscine* walls, poster-boy for the new nobility
our parents have secured.

By nightfall we'll be drunk as lords and hatching
desperate schemes of co-authored wealth, the cicadas hammering
distantly away like tills,

but now a bee razors the air along
my ear, and I scare as though caught in the midst of a low
and dirty act.

The handyman feeds the scrapheap. Your mother
sidles through the gate, trilling our dinner plans and tidings from Minèrve.
Love, I have to jump

and break the water, the better to hide
these stretch marks and the suspicion that in me you've made
a bad bargain.

from *Poetry Wales*

Waves

◇　◇　◇

The sea is a misunderstanding
we have to go through in order to make sense,
like the word for the loss of a word.
It leaves a sense of having left,
through which silence leaks.

What waves are reopening nightly is
the senseless apparatus of an eye.
If you live in a house made of thought
you nod in the silence the sea makes.

Sometimes we open
another book, its leaves are like nets.
A plane is losing its thread,
wave-woven sand shelves under the toes.

The feeling comes numbly at night.
Ears are only channels for this,
the imprecision at the end of your
limbs. You feel giddy to look.

Look through your impression of water,
the evolution you drag inside you.
Poe-lipped polyps lens and tense
to sense the same body inside this one.
Their homeland is brine,
the gull-lulling greys of its waves.

Lip-read the sea rolling in pain. See
such children it sucks like a sweet.

The pebbles are frantic under them.

from *Shadowtrain*

Young Pterodactyl

◇ ◇ ◇

But we almost didn't notice it, folded into its wings
on the pathway, under rusty leaves.
Don't touch, it will perish if we acknowledge it, I said
but instead you wrapped it in your jumper
and held it in your arms.

We carried it home, a parcel of angles and nerves
and if anyone saw us, I couldn't tell.
The beak was a blunted eggtooth, the rubbery feet
curled inwards the same as a baby's,
but this was new to us.

That night I could think only of its hopelessness,
its eyes, two huge questions in its head.
I built a crate for it to live in, hammering each nail
with a promise to let it go
when the time came.

The next morning I held it, flapping inside my arms
like a dishtowel, while you offered it bits of steak.
It wouldn't eat them and its beak
closed on us for a whole day and night
and we were worried.

Eventually it warmed to us, knuckle-walking on its wings.
We shook our heads—was anything quite like
this knock-kneed little bonebird
we'd decided on keeping
for our own amusement?

We loved it with our eyes closed, simply, too much,
now it has grown and shivered off its down
to reveal the first scale.
Tonight it is enormous as a mood
roosting over our heads.

from *Stop Sharpening Your Knives*

Later

◇ ◇ ◇

after the work stopped
       water filled the quarry pit
(just a kerb of raw pink limestone showing
by the cherry-ripe DANGER DEEP WATER sign)
           then it was available for light

and for transients, drawn
       by its glint from the sky.
The landscaped car park bays are emptying
in the all-at-once late afternoon, a safely-gathered-in
          of scattered child cries for the night.

A small flock (black
       snags I can't name
in a reflected satin blue) is intent on itself,
its scoots, squabbles and lulls, as busy as a shopfloor
         at being the species they are

dip-and-shrugging and
       frisking themselves. One
stands up, almost, on the water, up-and-un-
ruffling wings of spray like (from here, with low sun
         behind) those of a larger

brighter bird than itself
       which is also itself
extended into space around it, the sensible
world. *Itself* . . . Yes, maybe that's what *self* is, not
         a tight-inside-us nub

but what we are, thrown
          out and off, un-self-seen,
once-for-all, betraying even as it leaves us
our position, giving itself (don't you long
                    to say 'gladly?') away

from *Poetry London*

A Butterfly in the British Museum

◇ ◇ ◇

Smuggled in on a schoolgirl's cuff,
its brushed wings dusting
the cabinet edges—agate seals

and scarabs, a charlatan's scrying
crystal and the turquoise teeth
of an Aztec skull. Spinning

to kneel, she shrugs loose
her knapsack, scrabbling
for sketchbook and pen,

when suddenly her wrist blossoms,
takes flight, meets itself
in a ricochet of glare—

its hieroglyphs ghosting
into cartouched tombs.
For an instant, the mystery

of the living and beauty of the dead
flutter in the glass; impulsive
lenses zoom *too late!, too late!*

as the soul of a doodling girl
vibrates to the sky-light's deep,
unpinnable blue.

from *PN Review*

The Ambition

◇ ◇ ◇

after Rabelais

The tide being out, I traipsed through dehydrated eelgrass and the chopped warm
salad of the shallows, and then the Atlantic breached me part by part.

If my knees knocked it was two flints striking
My skin shagreen
My thorax a corset compressed rib by rising rib
My fingerprints finely-carved trilobites of the shore
My fine motor skills as good as any butterwort's
My nailbeds pale flukes: lemon soles or witches
My blood a thick slow scrawl of crude
A raw kebab my vertebrae strung on the spinal cord
My throat a maypole for eel-grass
My retinas red rags to bulls
My nose and ears sympathetic remora
My pigtail a withered stipe or shaw
My moles and freckles rising spores
My sweat-glands like mud-buried lugworms
My friendly bacteria Vichysoisse
My urine a strong hot tisane
My tongue and lips sweetmeats seasoned by an infinite cruet
My sphincter the knot in a balloon poodle
My brain-pan a shovel of quenched ash
My cerebellum a baitball

If seals mobbed the shallows it was only for my liver
If my kidneys complained it was Bert and Ernie
If I floated it was spatchcock, trussed on the rack of the swell
If I expressed myself it was liquids and vowels
If my knuckles were cracked it was for their rich marrow

My pituitary a pair of repelling magnets
My name sticks and sinking stones
My musculature like dispersing cirrus
My children a cloud of clumped alfabeti
My mouth a burst ripe vacuole

from *Magma*

Hitodama (人魂 or 'Human Soul')

◇ ◇ ◇

Fetch candle. Death fire. Falling star.
Ignis fatuus. Will o' the wisp. Wraith.
Sea spirit. Doppelganger. Friar's lantern.
Soft phosphorescence on the water.

When a soul fails to cross the thin gap
into death, one foot stuck fast in the body
of a man, this blue-white ball of flame
trails over the spit swamp like a trick,
its tail a silhouette of the dead's face.

Do not stare out onto the wet darkness.
Bottle your eyes, blow out the candle.
Forget your instincts, follow your map.
For to see the *hitodama* is an omen:
you will lose your soul forever in the fen.

from *Edinburgh Review*

Valediction

◇ ◇ ◇

We two like a parted compass? No, not really—since
we are moving, since the world is moving. The sun

throws shadows of us; you and I trace lines that do not correspond.
What to do? Wide-eyed on caffeine for days? Drunk at noon?

Hold still for a moment. It starts to rain. So there's nothing
can be done anyway. Not the shopping or gardening.

Plates gleam in rows on the sideboard. Is it raining there?
Do you leave continental beauties to shelter from the rain?

Leave the house. This is good solid air. It plunges a course
to my lungs. Stand up straight. Stop beneath a streetlight.

The weekend laid out—a mahogany table—I know
where it is; I know where you are. When it rains

the earth smells like it's been there for years.

from *The Rialto*

Sonnet

◇ ◇ ◇

The vast pumpkin-coach sprays ochre dust
on the finely-etched grain: how many brassy-gleaming
coins flung to clatter amongst the crowds' gurgling
clishmaclaver, how many phosphorescent
torques hung . . . ? No will's as strong
as a cloud in which a voice mumbles, engulfing
its audience with an adolescent strum, or better yet
(hoarsely now) the pyx-bound diarchy propped
upon a burnished palm! Yet over the bristling
ice-chafed land the foghorns disperse, eventually running out
of twine; the cliffs lean and shift like pale passengers
squashed against the pane; the sea shirrs
against itself, hissing, unfurled, of its irreversible wane:—
standing here, I count myself, count myself again.

from *PN Review*

from *Errant*

◊ ◊ ◊

Off-centre in the centre of my life—
that's how it's always been: the ideals slip
away, the mastery will not arrive;
while habits fix, reforms refuse to grip.
A daoist vegetarian, too hip
to compromise the future with his vote;
a dope who, vindicated by the trip,
still couldn't tell the ocean from the boat,
got off his floating world, grew backwards to
the family as art, then failed to follow through.

Inventing the vocation in the Haugh,
that cross-roads where a B-road crossed the Urr,
rewired my brain into an anxious loch,
a broth of hypochondria, a blur
through which an ageing doctor wasn't sure
but thought she saw a tumour like a trout.
A night in hospital is not a cure
nor are two tests, then three more months of doubt
before the scan, but as the auld man laughed
at midnight in the worried ward, "They'll wheech us aff

and cover us in concrete." Nurses drew
a conference of curtains round his bed
and left us dreamless, lucid, hopeless, new,
in transit through the outlands of the dead.
Mature art meant the carapace was shed—
no aping others' genius, claiming nous
while acting like a faithless infant ned:
there was a child that stanzas wouldn't house

but I could hope to father; a career—
the teacher first learns how to leave the House of Fear.

Those nurses and our muses are the same:
they've dealt with us and with the likes of us
before, grand vanities and little shame –
sometimes vice versa, but, whatever, thus
it is with these vile bellies: just adjust
perspective on Parnassus, say the pines,
and watch us go—first flesh, then rot, then dust;
they overlook the final twitch of lines,
footless as snakes who treat their tails as teats.
Go mouthy or go mute—you go, they wash your sheet.

When I was on the Low Road's darkest patch,
a baby girl upon my shoulders, the cats' eyes
that should have lit its single track all scratched
out by anxiety, I recognised
them as my ancestors', their colour prised
from black and white, my gran's old greeny blue
made cataracted marbles, and surmised
I must still be in hospital, not through
its lidless night, not yet, not waking up
for months, just learning where you go without a map.

When I was on the Silk Road's lowest stretch
between the two oases' green-tiled tombs,
Peach Blossom Paradise beyond our reach
behind the Kunlun's range of grim jade gums
all fanged with ice, our livers had no homes,
our hangovers were nomads and our lights
revolved within our bellies, since our bones
were swopped for sharp dust-devils—in that night
I saw the frightening place I'd visited
back in the Haugh, though like the country of the dead,

was never there at all, instead it was
a Helicon, that habitation next
to clarity, awake to lack of cause
and simple as cold water's lens, its flex
of sunlight in cupped palms. Placed outside text,

you watch that scorpion beside your foot
and see it has no goals, is unperplexed
and ready as a sickness. There's no route
that leads to anywhere but here; no shame,
no game: the Silk Road and the Low Road are the same.

from *The Warwick Review*

Deil Tak The Hinmaist

◊ ◊ ◊

'I think ye ocht t' pit the pillywinkies on t' him..'

The girt yett kickit in, an lo!—they liggit: *scummers o pots*
an skelpers o cuddies; jaws that cleikit, rhymes that reikit; Kerr's Pink
tatties biled in their jaickets; deedle-dabblers in cytoplasm; virtual
realtors swickin an swyvin; daddy-lang-legs; dirlin Dodies;
hoodie-craws cracklin fae the tippy-taps o trees:

> Deid-loss or Daidalos
> fit's it gaan tae be?

Pooshin pumpers, coonter-jumpers, cairpet fitters birslin wi a moo-fae
o tacks; tomcats; corncrakes; shilly-shally sharn shifters; couthy
bicuspids; aa the wee glisterin anes; aa them that wid grudge ye one jow
o the bell.

The neist yett swung, syne mair wis kythit: tethered tups,
draigelt yowes; the slalom loons fae Dandruff Canyon; wheepers
o candy-floss; footerin futtrets; the hee-haw-hookum o hystet hizzies;
foosty fowk lik Finnan haddies; Buckie blaavers wi the full wecht o
blaw.

Shouther tae the third yett, an jist as ye micht expeck: sornars
an sooks; herriers an haverers; gran chiels in blue corduroy, fantoosh
wifies; r.p. flannel dinkers; parkins, merkins; secont-sichtit seannachies
wi hunkies clappit t' their snoots; flunkeys; junkies; buglers; shooglers;
Methuselahs wi nips an tucks; trashtrie shotten aff the shelf.

> As douce a set o creepy-crawlies
> as ye're ivver like t' see.

Here-am-ur; hempseed; fushionless tail-toddle:
Daith's on the fussle lik the win throw the widdy.

Roon the corner, an doon the stair: polyglot thrapple-stappers;
chirpy chairmers; mingers an moochers; bracken for brakfast, neebors
for lunch. Lest bit nae least: flees in putty, wersh wicks in seas o wax.

Coda: Scoor it if ye fancy intil ae muckle plum duff—
plooms, suet, orange peel—simmert slaw an slaistert
in slices, faa's t' say it winna lest for years?

from *Gutter*

GLOSSARY:

Hinmaist: hindmost; *ocht*: ought; *pilliwinkies*: finger or thumb screws, an instrument of torture; *girt yett*: great gate; *liggit*: lay; *skelpers*: strikers, whippers; *cuddies*: horses; *cleikit*: caught, hooked on to; *reikit*: stank; *tatties*: potatoes; *deedle-dabblers*: dilettantes; *dirlin*: reverberating; *Dodie*: George; *fit*: what; *gaan*: going; *swickin an swyvin*: cheating and screwing; *daddy-lang-legs*: crane flies; *hoodie-craws*: hooded or carrion crows; *pooshin*: poison; *birslin*: bristling; *moo-fae*: mouthful; *couthy*: cozy, homely; *glisterin*: shiny; *sharn*: dung; *jow*: peal; *neist*: next; *syne*: then, subsequently; *kythit*: revealed; *tup*: ram; *draigelt yowes*: bedraggled ewes; *loons*: lads; *footerin*: hesitant, exasperating; *futtrets*: weasels or stoats; *hee-haw-hookum*: an indeterminate mischief; *hystet*: hoisted; *hizzies*: women-folk; *foosty*: fusty, mouldy; *fowk*: folk; *Finnan haddies*: a type of smoked haddock; *blaavers*: braggarts, boasters; *wecht*: weight; *blaw*: wind; *shouther*: shoulder; *sornars*: importunate scroungers; *sooks*: flatterers; *herriers*: robbers, plunderers; *haverers*: gabblers, people speaking nonsense; *gran chiels*: VIP's; *fantoosh*: extra fancy; *wifies*: women; *r.p.*: 'received pronunciation', posh spoken; *parkins*: large, round, ginger and oatmeal biscuits; *merkin*: a pubic wig (some say) or the sine qua non; *seannachies*: wise men; story-tellers; *snoots*: snouts; *shooglers*: shakers; *trashtrie*: rubbish; *douce*: proper, respectable; *fushionless*: limp; vapid; *tail-toddle*: intercourse; *fussle*: whistle; *widdy*: wood; *thrapple*: throat; *stappers*: stoppers, stuffers; *mingers*: ugly wasters; *moochers*: cadgers; *flees*: flies; *wersh*: dull; scoor: scour, scrape; *duff*: pudding; *plooms*: plums; *slaw*: slow; *slaistert*: slathered; *faa*: who; *lest*: last.

SARAH JACKSON

Light Over Ratcliffe

◊ ◊ ◊

The turnip field is waterlogged. We're sinking
the further we get from the track. Eye whites

of root vegetables lift from the black loam
and I dunk the green tops in their graves,

more wet than mud, the whole field swallowing
and I'm glad. I want the earth to take me in.

It'll be dark soon enough. The horses are napping.
The furrows lead us over a grass-topped bridge

and back onto a railway track that rips open
the gut of the field. Tripping the sleepers

we follow it home, hearing the haunt
of a train shunt the space between us.

Passing a copse that criss crosses through dusk
we near the farm with the dogs. He twists at last

to look at me, but his eyes slip over the top
of my head, and his smile carefully unfastens.

He turns me as in bed. A vast white glare
breathes over the towers, a luminous cloud

lifting and smelting our faces, and in the instant
it takes to reach him, I am already blind.

from *Staple*

The Retired Eunuch

◇ ◇ ◇

Today I crashed my last wedding, hung up
my bells; kissed goodbye to my maracas.
From now, I will dance only for myself,
choose turquoise stones from the village bazaar
and walk between the grass and the green wheat.
I will wear a yellow turban and striped shirt
and when I draw my pension, will put aside
enough for the silver stilettos I saw in the shop
in Chandigarh to be worn on the anniversary
of my mother's death. At night I will wear
the white headdress shaped like a swan,
dream of the City Beautiful and Lucky Ali
with his denim shirt and Dean Martin eyes.
In spring when my skin is still as pale
as the palace of the ambassador, I will walk
the high paths, pick the yellow flower
and feel rain on my feet; I will not speak of the past.
In my last days, I will play at high volume
the big hits of Daler Mehndi, the Bhangra King,
learn the sarangi and once every year journey
to the shores of the Bay of Bengal. My soul,
I give to the stars, my eyes to the orphans.
I will leave behind nothing but yesterday.

from *Iota*

Hennecker's Ditch

◊ ◊ ◊

I stood at the station
like the pages of a book
whose words suddenly start to swim.

Wow. The rain. Rose beetles.

Formal lines of broad–leaved
deciduous trees
ran the length of the platform.

Ickira trecketre stedenthal, said the train.
Slow down please, said the road.
Sometimes you get lucky, said the estate agent
        onto his mobile phone,
it all depends on the seller.

Dear Circus,
Past the thicket, through the window,
the painéd months are coming for us—

See the bluff, the headland, announcing
the presence of water.
See the moths . . .

The trees walk backwards into the dark.

Hello? Hello? The snow
comes in sobs.
Dogs sob.
Cars sob across town.

Dear Circus,
When you found me
I was a rickety house.

There was a yellow light and a blanket
        folded up on the stoep
and the yellow light — *Dear Circus* —
was a night-blooming flower.

We pushed a chest of drawers against the door.
It's nice now that the corridor's empty.
A necklace. Vacant. Light wrecked the road.

Dear Circus,
We took off our clothes
and did cocaine for three weeks.

The washing machine shook so badly
that a man asleep four floors down reached out
        to hold it:
Shut that dirty little mouth of yours . . .

Hennecker's Ditch.

You'll never find it, he said over dinner,
a black lobster and bottle of vinegar,
unless, unless . . .

Blackened,
the dog tilts his head from beneath
        the canopy of the Karoo tree.
Look at my face, he said. Can you see what
        I'm thinking?

A red jersey. Bot bot bot.
Séveral breezes.
Boats on the water were moving at different speeds.
The baker took a portable radio
        into the garden
to listen to the cricket
in the shade of the bougainvillea.

Tick-a-tick-ooh, tick-a-tick-ah.
It was cloudy but hot. We were moving
    as shadows.

Three times he came upstairs and made love to her
then went back down and read his book.
The air was blood temperature
    and the consistency of blood.

Look at my face, he said.
I see you. I see you. I see you
    in our murky bath
I see you in our black and white bath like a cat.

Barbed wire around the fisheries.
A letter from the municipality
Come closer, sir. Step into my office.

Above the harbour, tin roofs and cranes.
Henry? he said.
Hello? Henry? he said.
What's been happening in Dog Town these days?
The Audi keys lay heavy on the table.
Aaaaah Henry, he said. How wonderful it is
    to see you.
The mists came down.
The moon was bright.
Collectors searched the night market
    with flashlights, and the wind outside,
with its slight chill, howled.
Henry, the breezes—they bolt across the open market
like meatballs, Henry,
like windmills, Henry,
like policemen, Henry, apprehending criminals . . .

A man in a collared shirt put a cigarette
    to his mouth
and looked at his watch.
And what happened then?
He wore a street hat. He wore a street hat and
    carried a belt over one arm.

And what happened afterwards?

Tell her . . . I think he has given up.
Tell her . . . I know now, this is what I've been afraid of
    all my life.

He closed the door and came in.
He closed the door and the sound of the bathwater dimmed.

Thirty-one back gardens.
Thirty-one back gardens overlooking
    the backs
of thirty-one houses.
Thirty-one houses looking out over the sea.
And the sea (of course it was) was marbled
    and contorting.

Are you sleeping?—Yes.
Figures in yellow mackintoshes make their way
    along the coastal path.
And what then, what then if I were to ask,
How much longer?
If I were to say, How much further?
It's just—
I have used up all my reserves.

There was a yellow light
and a blanket folded up on the stoep.
The light was burning dimly now.
By that time,
the light had begun to flicker.

He opened the door and fastened
    his lonely shadow
and she fastened hers
and sat on the chair.

I think we are in the middle, aren't we.
He said, I think we may be.
We certainly aren't at the beginning anymore.

The moon was acting strangely.
The moon was moving fast.
It was cloudy but hot.
Electricity cables gathered round a pole
like the roof of a marquee.

He wore a gold vagina on his chest.
He had gold lining on the flaps of his jackét.
She lay her head against the window and sang a song
    by Silvio Rodriguéz
wearing ten gold balls on a chain around her neck.

Dear Circus,
Sometimes we are just so full of emotion.

And what happened then?
And what happened afterwards?
Chicken bones and Pick 'n Pay receipts.
We were moving as shadows.
And the only light
        was the light from the bakery.

A lampshade swings above the window.
Tick-a-tick-ooh, tick-a-tick-ah
We have no history.
Nothing has passed between us.

A hundred years pass like this.
Dear Circus,
I need to see more glass!
I need to see more glass!
This has to be more gentle.

from *PN Review*

Collusion

◊　◊　◊

We'd wake to find the place
strange. Even some treeless
crossroads in the back-end
of nowhere could, in a flash,
change: famous for a second
then synonymous with loss.

To commune, we knelt in packs
at altar rails on velvet pads
but still each pose was unalike:
head up; head down; dead tired;
frail; some arthritic twinge
or nerve trapped in the hip.

You might see from the aisle
the price stickers exposed
on the soles: mine, outsized,
were a man's practical brogues
from Eastwoods' fire sale.
All ceremony is a hoax.

In bandit country the blackface
and cheviot, damp-fleeced, raddled,
wander unaware of entering
and exiting the great stone rings
archaeologists uncover, claim
are like enough memorial.

from *Poetry London*

Coal End Hill Farm 1962

◇　◇　◇

I don't remember the Beanley orra–man,
his boots down the lonnen black as a wet day, his caravan
under a butchered elm's imaginary wingspan,
rusted, cantankerous: *"all that can's been done,"*
my mother said, then, low, *"he's God's own one."*
I can't recall his singing of the Kingdom come,
or whispering from underneath his hands
"if my soul the Lord should take," or how he crept away
like Billy Blin, awake long hours before the blackbirds, eager to begin
carving off a dead lamb's skin to roll one barely-living in
under a dazed ewe, force tongue to tit, tit to tongue:
mole-blind he'd move, from east to western sun, more whole
in his Gomorrah than the doucest thing, but slow,
immortal, helpless as his beasts to conjure up tomorrow.

from *Northwords Now*

Kingfisher

◇　◇　◇

It is true, it does nest with the opening year, but not on the waters
—CHARLES OLSON

How do you describe the blue you've never seen?

I was fixing the biting muzzles of mitts to the Boy's fingers

　　you saw

　　　　—the tail-less hologram shoot its bib of ore—

I was holding the Boy from the lagoon-green underbreeze of the lake

　　　　　—the blue flex shook green its Atlantic dorsal—

I was persuading the Boy that faces in puddles were not the only ones to
　　　　　　　　　　　　　　　　　　　understand him

　　　　—the savage-buddha ball-bearing for digested fishbone—

I was hauling the Boy's knees from the altar of logpools

　　　　　—the blast of Bunsen make shrift its short fuel—

I was kneading the yeast-kisses he tossed to Canada geese

　　　—an azure lizard shed January's skin—

I was searching a path for the Boy's alchemy of chance in gold grass

　　—the pixelated dash from Victorian taxidermists—

I was pushing the Boy in euphorics towards the A-roads of futurist
fire-services

        —the damsel-blue hunter thrust its mollusc-lance—

(I read, that night, *only the righteous see the kingfisher*)

    hours later, the Boy asleep,
    his consciousness given back to dreams
       —a gale to the windchimes—
    his exhausted limbs lit by the trip-switch of pulse—

    the righteous one said, as I drifted to dark
      —said the one word—*kingfisher*—
    and I caught his blue—pulled back from the only place I'd ever
seen him

from *The Rialto*

Beverly Downs

◊ ◊ ◊

That first morning, the shock of children's voices
impossibly far away, carried as if across a meadow.
I had forgotten schoolyards, shopping centres, choice,
that there was a solid life around the shadow
cast about me, the shadow I'd become,
or such a thing as time decreed by something
neutral as a clock or the rhythm of an urban day.
Banked against the wall, houses, mute, their backs turned
as if in judgement. Waiting, I only knew the grey
of snow to come, the chill of being stranded, not
what was possible, a gift, or needing to be earned.
A year on, and that lost figure is a vacuum
waiting to envelop me if ever I forget
that the brightest uplands are on the very rim
of disaster. For now, it is enough to have seen the wall
from the placid, ordered slope of Beverly Downs,
the luxury still of a clear head at noon
and the odd exhaustion of having slept too well.

from *Envoi*

Sleeping Hermaphrodite

◊　◊　◊

Asleep? I'm watching you through my lids.
This isn't easy, tracking your nebulous shape
while you assess my neck's turn, slide
down to smooth cleavage, tummy, waist

then encounter what's stashed below my thigh.
Here I am, unveiled as arguable,
a mishmash of harbour and ship — the stay
in thought when all ideas are possible.

I'm everything yet deeply ill-equipped
for solitude. What I need to know
is whether you ache to prise free

the ankle I've left loosely wrapped
in a sheet. Singlespeak is boring. Let's talk toes
and honey. Come on, nosey boy. Surprise me.

from *Poetry London*

House Clearance

◇ ◇ ◇

Turn the key: note how the emptiness accumulates
as you come in; how by being here at all you seem to add to it,

until it fills the corridor with that fermented stasis
you both disturb and add to as you move. Pass

through a second door, a portal of stirred air,
ignore the rooms to left and right and take the stairs,

your shoes dislodging dust that billows
up in tiny detonations. You're walking underwater,

the silt explodes beneath your feet; at first you think you'll drown
but what's flashing through your mind in one

slow-motion scattering of greys is not your own life but theirs.
No matter that you still can't breathe—that's how it's always

been in here: even the nothingness is thick as blotting paper
on which their shapes have spread like ink—must, damp,

the outline of a body sketched in mothballs and almost-
memory. The furniture is ghostly beneath the sheets

but the missing pictures are still there, outlined
in frames of dirt on squares of wall now white as bone

surprised beneath the skin. You were in every one of them.
Now you're the last flame in the grate:
Hamlet in his theatre of shadows, their embers at your feet.

from *Agenda*

My Life as a B Movie

◇ ◇ ◇

The back seat of a New York cab is where we'd meet,
with just a dash of slapstick, clashing as we slid
from either door, preoccupied, our eyes still fixed
on sleek, no-heart ex-lovers stalking off
in just-beginning snow; and then we'd turn,
contrite and awkward (bravely blinking tears)
to spark a chivalrous exchange of "*No, you take it,*"
"*Oh, but I insist,*" until, on cue,
the twinkly driver couldn't help but turn
and ask our destinations, which, of course,
would come out miles away, and just a block apart:

that's how it would start. And then, the usual:
all heavily-foreshadowed, third-act fallings-out
would spring from missing facts, or conversations
wrong-half-overheard, or just some ancient trauma
selflessly concealed to spare the innocent
or simply the forgiven, all depending on
how hurt and sainted I was written up to be;

except, of course, I'd not be cast as me,
but rather as the taller, older, plain best friend
who counsels staff and customers alike
from aft the glove counter at Saks or Bloomingdales;
who warmly offers kleenex, gawky shoulders and solicitude
with wisecrack acumen at any time of night
over cherry pie and coffee in some rainy diner;

and when the happy-ever-after tacks its backdrop sheet
of closing sunset here at ninety-fifth and Broadway,
and our loved-up leads high-tail for JFK
in a Yellow Cab that's driven by *guess who!*

while neighbours wave and hug on fire escapes
and grumpy Mr Bachman from the corner store pursues
with sheafs of roses, all disarmed and sappy,
and then we *fade to black*, I'll turn aside and take
the crushed and muggy subway back uptown
to that grey apartment the camera never sees,
the spooling lines of credits rolling over me
like ripples on a pond in which I've drowned already
somewhere in another town, another movie.

from *Poetry London*

And then there will be no more nonsense

◇   ◇   ◇

And then there will be no more nonsense
and you will tell her about that evening

when you stopped in the dusk at the edge
of the grass you had cut that afternoon

and looked back to where you had just sat
on the patio eating the meal she had cooked

and saw how blessed it all appeared if someone
had watched from where you stood.

from *The Rialto*

Of Other Spaces (Tate St. Ives)

◇ ◇ ◇

i.

You are a green place
    wild rice and marsh birds
flying the blue horizon
    of the hundred thousand things I will never know
a blur, or curvature
    three times and trembling
against stillness whose
    stone asks after your tongue
the moment where you breathed
    and stopped, a winding cut from the sheet of the world

ii.

Did my lover make the curtain? Yes. Between
sculpting and the sea. She made certain. She

occurs in this room. The empty cup. The stillness
of the day. She resonates, is the thickness of paint.

Is white. Yes. My memories are this blue. The sea's
particular invention: to want to see through blue,

whose translucence salts the eye. Taste it. I have never
thought of the sea as my lover. Never thought of her

as a wall. But there it is. And another, and another.
The emptying room. Blazing full.

from *Agenda*

Rats

◊ ◊ ◊

Here, everything runs on time. And here,
everything is clean. So much so, that a divorce
might be granted if either the husband,

or his wife, should make it to the platform
a few seconds late. Or a love affair might be ended
if either the other man, or the other woman,

should forget to brush their teeth. And yet,
here, as everywhere else, there are rats. You can see
them watching, enviously, from the side

of the tracks. You can see them polishing
their teeth underneath the neon sign of the local pharmacy.
Or you can see them, as I did, on a summer's night,

in the middle of a city, strolling, unashamedly,
through a park, with one eye on the eighteenth century
palace, and the other on the main chance.

from *Gutter*

Pluvialis

◇ ◇ ◇

Lovers lounge, oblivious.
                A fisherman casts
his frayed patience
upon the afternoon. Beyond them

a last flock of waders, at the end
of their strange alchemy, drab of winter
swapped for waistcoats in full-dress black,

gold-leaf mantles worn lightly. Clockwork toys,
they whirr and
                stutter on,
and here and there one leapfrogs the loose huddle,
the lead changing constantly.

They shape to startle
with each shadow overhead, each slam
of a distant car door, each soft explosion
of the courting couple's laughter; and birds lift into the air

but just fail to carry off the rest of the flock, drop
back to earth, false starts only serving to defer
                      the inevitable,
the muted percussion of the first drops
then the hard drench, and a moment's intense

silence   before they are gone,

gone as one, air dense with the stretched iambs
of their calls, flickering across the cloudbank

like pain or pleasure across your grey eyes

until finally   at distance
a thin strand unties

                    then unites again,
all of them rising in slow, wide circles
like smoke from a sacrifice,
each bird dissolving into the storm
or each drop of rain carried away
on the wings of the plovers.

                    from *Iota*

The Apple Farmers' Calendar

◇ ◇ ◇

And after all these years she wears
a skin of dirt. He didn't take her
down at the millennium,
too fond of letting his eye run
to her pale belly,

a quince compared
to stripy watermelons that block
the light beside the dented pewter
bowl weighed low by a pumpkin
heaved on the scales.

The woman at his stall
haggles for a better price
while, inches from the plank
where he wraps figs
in fig leaves, Eve regards him

with her usual calm.
The apple in her hand
is coated in a powdering of dust,
swirled by the growers' trucks
that labour up Mount Pilion.

Delicate, she offers it
time after time. If now and then
she slips, her painted toes
just touch the bluish paper
he keeps to parcel eggs.

from *New Welsh Review*

Short-hold

◊ ◊ ◊

This is the gap before territory,
    before the first fight, the first sex.

The black cat knows it, twitching his tail
    on the wrong lawn.

This is the time when our luck might stray—
    the syllable *flit* swoops through the trees,

leaves behind reminder
    after red reminder.

Even this lamplight's provisional,
    tomorrow may shine from a different window;

our lives are still fragile
    wrapped in old headlines and stars.

How empty the white bookshelves are,
    how easily tipped . . .

weightless the walls of clocks, pictures, mirrors . . .
    I stand at the open door, calling . . .

Meanwhile you've lit the difficult boiler.
    All night its steady breathing fills the kitchen

like the sleep of a new-born
    we haven't yet named.

from *Mslexia*

Delicacy

◊   ◊   ◊

The château would have been beautiful though melancholy
if the birdscarer had not gone off from five a.m.
with the dreadful crack of a gun, every nineteen minutes
and fourteen seconds, in the name of plums.
A plum in almost every stage of development;
an infant plum, a gothic emo one, a full-blown blowsy plum,
an elderly plum, an almost-gone-dotty plum.
As in some tedious lesson we were instructed in plums
mi-cuit, cuit from hoardings, from touristy hand-outs.
And on return, in the corner of one's eye, up pops
an Agen plum in a West London delicatessen!
At Christmas, a box of same plums in the post.
There is only so much conspiracy one can buy into.
But lying in the bath feeling the edges of my body wrinkle,
I'm sure I can feel my cardiac plum darken.
It shocks me into wondering
if the moon waxes above the long drive?
Whether a fawn still comes to drink at the swimming pool?
And if the boys who walked off and away, did so
carrying as a souvenir, a homely black wadding:
sun-proof, rain-proof, though ultimately perishable.

from *Smiths Knoll*

Logo

◇ ◇ ◇

I,
St Edmund's bloodshot bell-clap, Jack
o' the clock, Jack smite-the-clock, Southwold
Jack, tell the hours in axe-song,
garbed in rolled-iron
echo, speak with raised right arm.

Blyth Jack, tide-knight, I've seen the ebb,
faces of saints
scratched to the grain, the anglian fleece
pitched spraywards — Dunwich and its woolgold
gone to the cod,
Suffolk turned

nuclear. In the fruit-light
of stained glass I
sing all this and silver plate
Southwold in a hammerstruck dome,

this town, my untimed first person,
smelted to ingots.

from *Fuselit*

Only Here On Earth

◊ ◊ ◊

"Earth is the region of the fleeting moment.
Will I have to go, like the flowers that perish?
    Will nothing remain, not even my songs?
    Is it only here on earth we come to know
our faces?" So wrote the teenage prince
exiled to Huexotzinco. Boughs of the pecan
    tree, flash of a flycatcher's wing, indigo
    wool in grey spice of a Tepanec rug.

Smoke rises over Mount Atloyan like a mirror.
    Distant melodies, clay flute and ocarina,
and that tricksy pass from cello to viola
    in the first-time-bar of the minuet
andante as a disciplined scholar.

There's no other world. Feather gloves
in a patch of sun on parquet floor.
    The perfect moment comes to us
    in its own time, planting bulbs for spring,
hearing the buzz of a stranger's orange press
and purring mill of coffee in the kitchen.
    Laying the table, hunting four-
    tined forks in the chaos of a cutlery drawer.

from *New Welsh Review*

California

◊   ◊   ◊

Its colour—gold—recalls the sunlight and the mother lode
glinting, that precious, punctured vein through Amador
and Calaveras County. The shuttle-woven Szechuan silk
brocade will lead me to this afternoon in Chinatown,
turning in my guidebook to 'Celestials'—Chinese railroad labourers
powering their way through stone, and reaching only stone.
A purse will do, a souvenir of leeching currency,
the blood that drives the heart of a machine of skilled machinists.
These strands, employed now, constitute a thing.
I'll buy this empty purse because it's beautiful and broke.

from *Poetry London*

Lapse

◇ ◇ ◇

The Greyhound is late. I've been fast
asleep too long to know why, but the man
beside me—Chinese—tells me what time it is.

He turns to the back-lit maze of his phone, taps
a geometry of buttons, gets lost in an exchange
about auditions and lost opportunities. I look

across the aisle: the big guy with the *Yankees*
cap has struck up a dialogue with the Polish
woman beside him. Her dark eyebrows arch—

an eager pair—in synch under her blond hail; I can
tell she's open; so is he, but he's fearful, hasn't
yet learnt the curved asymmetry of lust. There is

already a lapse between her keenness, his lean
and the speed of his initiative. Somebody should
tell him that if the lapse grows any longer

the door of chance will close—snap in
his face. It's already too late. The bus is
drifting into Harlem, Connecticut a distant memory:

I hear him say, *Excuse me*; he calls his Mom. A pink
rose blooms on the woman's cheek, she looks
outside. I hang my head, exhale, and close

my eyes. The man beside me snaps his phone shut.

from *South Bank Poetry*

Hare

◊ ◊ ◊

You dreamed the field was a tin grid,
Latticed with running hares, March-mad and stargazy,
Their quick jolts the firing of neurons.

At other times you meet him alone:
That long face, the dowsy parting at the mouth,
A suggestion of teeth; lecherous, repulsive, somehow
Irresistible. *Witch.*

And he was there in pinstripes,
Haunches drawn out on their pivot,
Leaning over your shoulder at the wedding party,
Those fine ears folded smooth down his back,
Complacent. Smug. Buck-sure.
His yellow eye met yours, knowing
You could do nothing. You thought:

I'll have you, you suave bastard.

Find him in a field. He's gone
In one swift arterial pump.
                              Oh, he is a tease . . .

            He is the sidelong, sidling
And askance,
        So learn to see as Hare sees,
            Learn his steps,
Accept his invitation up to dance:
He'll stay that spring-heeled jolt if you keep time.
Walk in rings around him. Do not spare
            One glance towards the centre or he'll bolt.
See how a pattern's there, a coiled line:

Tighten up the circles, and each whorl
Will shave a sickle off the verticil.
        Pare away the moons. His labyrinth's
A unicursal round: with just one end,
        And just one track. He'll be waiting,
Slant-eyed jack, and prince
        Of tricks. Your part is fixed:

        A virgin going down,
        A widow coming back.

        from *The Rialto*

10 × 10

◊ ◊ ◊

for Judith

1. ORIGAMI

You are a folded deer quick-stepping
the bog-cotton muir of a how-to book.
Hind for the white hart whose leathery heart you have
smoothed to bleaching linen or a page
freshly rolled in the mill, I adore you

for every crease unironed in your nature.
Not for me the copper-bottomed überbeauties,
those bronzed denizens of the glossies
who are glazed like fine porcelain and just as vacant
as washed tins dropped in the recycling.

2. SUMMERTIME . . .

Backlit by a Balkan sunset, in your denim skirt
and well-worn sandals you sit by the water's edge:
it's a favourite snap of mine. The gloaming heckles
dark from the evening, turning the trees across the bay
to pig-iron sculptures of themselves. In that light,

your hair becomes a metonym for fire, as if
burnishing the air around to a deep bronze sheen;
your smile becomes a kiln for happiness. As if
we could can that for the years ahead! Still, while we're able,
let's linger in the moment's printed afterglow.

3. SHAGREEN

Imagine us old: wrunkled cowhide faces,
me in linen trousers at some summer festival,
one of us walking with a stick, both chatting
with the bittersweet, gentle irony of the aged,
all trace of copper faded from your hair.

Our younger heads, cast in bronze by a friend,
may occupy a prominent spot beside your Dutch vase,
prevailing over the tinpot fears of ageing
as we recall fondly the days of cheap paper,
inexpensive cotton and less heat.

4. THE RAVELLING

A certain group of flaxen-haired wee boys
has breached the doors of pre-school nursery.
We spy them through the railings and experience
a kick like power surging down the wires—.
Grief is no monolith. It's more like molten bronze

or a potsherd dug up in unexpected tilth.
It speeds like a tinfish out of sonar range.
It's a crack that can't be papered over
for long, a snapped thread left to hang,
a belt to scourge our each essay at happiness.

5. DOVETAIL JOINTS

I could never have lifted you over the threshold.
And let's not count the ways I've dropped the iron,
or mention the nail you hammered through a hot water pipe,
the sun screen I slaistered on well past its use-by. Let's not
enumerate the plates and bowls that clattered from our grasp

this past 10 year. That's all in the can. Instead,
I'm leafing through the future's wide extensions,
its beds replanted with pear trees and cotoneaster.
A suede-upholstered future, our coming years together
unfolding like a brand new pack of king-sized sheets.

6. FERROUS SULPHATE

Dark chocolate, Guinness and steamed asparagus.
Your thickened hair basting in the summer sun,
your skin not burnished, browned or slightly burnt.
Casseroles and other one-pot dishes sitting by the door.
Tinned apricots crowding the kitchen cupboards

as if on free prescription. Red books and birth certificates.
Fitted cot sheets, muslin squares and body suits.
My footwear worn from pounding the surrounding streets.
The linens on our whirligig and no space left for drying.
How mighty oaks we hope from little acorns now are growing.

7. SMALL CHANGE

Every red penny we save these days
is technically bronze, so nothing—not even
the humble piggy bank, or the chugger's
rattly plastic collecting tin—is quite
what it looks on paper. Nor are we

who we were when we first shared the sheets,
my kilt and sporran tossed with your dress,
the hotel linens wrapping us tight. But I
don't pine to buy those times back, not even though
what we've shared since then would temper steel.

8. COMING THIRD

Never was it gold or silver in the medal stakes.
Never bone china, always the bargain-basement crockery.
Never the full spectrum, always the tinnier speakers.
Always paper-thin ham instead of the juicier cuts;
static-filled synthetics rather than Egyptian cotton.

But now we're talking genuine Italian leather,
an Irish linen garment cut to fit just so,
African ebony inlaid with mother of pearl,
pure Ossetian free of loans and calques,
a sunstruck copper roof devoid of verdigris.

9. A Cut-Price Set of Crockery

Barely six months' use when the glaze cracked.
It felt as smooth as a fresh roll of kitchen foil,
an unsigned marriage certificate or
the new sheets on our first, rented bed but looked
more like withered shoes beneath museum glass.

We traced the daily strains with our dishtowels
and at the table over breakfast or dinner.
Iron sharpens iron it is written. We felt more like
a copper cup already turning green. But no:
we were a new-minted penny ready to shine.

10. Not Being the Woodsman of Oz

I once played the cowardly lion; a coward
not only in the script, whispered some who'd not
cottoned on — seeing how feart I was
of a playground leathering; of muddying my
clothes on the pitch; of the opposite sex — that courage

to weep could compensate. Bit of a cross to bear.
You had your crosses too, hard as nails and heavier.
They may mean you feel no Venus, but to me
you're a bronze shield cast by Vulcan or a new
earthenware goblet brimming with wine.

from *Gutter*

At First, the Only Concern is Milk, More or Less

◇　◇　◇

The baby wanted to be sure to reach us and came
with hair and no clothes. It's hardly surprising,
given the expedition. Good afternoon, we said.

The task is to think things up. We said words like:
What is not a strange place? and In the field, look!
the calf's devotion to a shapeless dairy surge.

This is how it would be if it were possible to forget
Europe and machine-stitched salopettes
and the smell of horses' noses and that the sky
is identical and words are identical.

A dumb love is in production. There is more to say
and less is said—least of all Mother, I cannot bear
to outlive you, which is all, really, that matters.
Sooner or later, it is actual trousers.

But where is the baby that's going to be
fooled one second by the words, think them relevant?
The nurses retreated to a disinfected lobby.
What else? She was a whole person, but small.

from *The Rialto*

Three Wishes

◊ ◊ ◊

What is it, then? A gold-yolked goose egg. A wilding bean-stalk.
　　The flatness of adulation. Being always young. The King, the Castle.
　Wheat stalks spindled to flash and twine.

Or a cozening, a camera snap that keeps you, fleece-wrapped and obdurate
　　as a retouched grave, a quiet pearl.

A thick sleep saved from thistling worry. A cleaned, thick-brick, gated place—
　　chrome and cream: control.
　Wired yammering to drown the sullen, rising sea.

Remember now, how the girl requested a tattooed point of light, a refined star—
　　woke to the blinding, ink-scrawled sail of space,
　　　　unbounded clusters, galaxies, cankering in her skin.

from *The Wolf*

Anti-circ

◇ ◇ ◇

The seat of artistic delight is between the shoulder blades . . . Let us worship the
spine and its tingle. Let us be proud of our being vertebrates, for we are vertebrates
tipped at the head with a divine flame. The brain only continues the spine: the
wick really goes through the whole length of the candle.
— VLADIMIR NABOKOV

Once I cracked *Lolita's* spine I found myself knee-deep in cheesecake;
my not-quite-fist unclenched, disclosed a wet cluster of blackberries.

Tennyson sank me into new car smell and a plush interior; the extras
threw roses and sweetmeats at my tinted glass across the cordon.

Reading Wilfred Owen I was Attenborough's thrilled silence
breathing round a bird whose syrinx learned to imitate a chainsaw;

the walls of my house crashed down in fumes of plaster and rayed glass
the night I dropped Naipaul. Joe Sacco's *Palestine* had the sad

dilapidated scent of changing rooms at school, plaques of mud
hole-punched by studs. Hopkins shone a walkable torchbeam

between rooftops; I felt gay as Mary Poppins then feared my mum
would drop me. Updike's prose flaunted the revealed

cleanliness of a girl's arse, its well-briefed sway up the stairs ahead;
and when I called up from the stacks Enoch Powell's uncut *First Poems*

her skilled tongue agitated my thankfully intact frenulum.

from *Horizon Review*

from *The Songs of Elisabeth So*

◊ ◊ ◊

I notice, now, that you've lost weight,
your hair is cropped, your body somehow smaller;
and square and unfamiliar, the lines of your dark suit

that show your gait has found a new lopsidedness,
the way my year-old son in shoes
adjusts his body to—and us the heart—

new freight
and finds me, as I wait here, only sad.

And I don't want, I find, those flowers
that used to spring up with your look,
then fade and darken at your passing.

The corridors are singing with your hurt.
Take songs away, take flowers away, take too
the gentle artfulness of your restraint.

You call me Elisabeth, which I like,
Elisabeth *So*, Elisabeth *Please*.
And you undress me in a dream.
And so you tease . . .

Forgive me these,
as your words, my love,
unhook, undo.
And do not move

until I'm there spelled out with you.
The bed is awake with us at last.

Your name is one
I will not speak.
Don't ask, don't ask me to.

Whose mouth is this in the roomy darkness,
Whose hand is this that flies with mine,
Who sails with me in the room in the darkness,
Whose body slips with mine through time.

Whose voice is this that calls me, calls me,
Who runs beside me like the wind,
Who holds me as the ocean pulls me,
Who holds me, word to word, a rhyme.

Tell me, what shall we do with this hour of abundance?
What shall we do with this hour of wonder?
What is the best way to sing our praise?

I ask and ask but you will not answer.

My mouth is yours—if only you'd answer,
To prove the darkness and the silence wrong.

We're out of season, out of luck,
the day pot-boiled to its unlovingness.
So go.

Like a wronged god, or a ghost.
I never wanted you.
For we are not a rhyming pair,

we are not in the one breath,
not the morning's sudden clear air.
We are not the surge

and swell, the ocean's rhythm;
we are
not even a plywood plane thrown up into the sky.

Ours is not this kind of gladness.
We're so unlovely and so small. Know that as
we lie together here.

It was the only blessing that I asked you for,
of leaving me unnoticed—
like the earth might tree seeds or a rouged leaf
in its fall.

Instead, you give me nothing,
catch me inside your coat
to see if you can catch my breath

steal me, my soul,

which slipping through me, in an instant, rises up
and hovers near the smell of you.

The thumping of your chest to which I'm otherwise immune
has left me on the wind's breath, now.
It was the blessing that I asked you for.

Instead you leave me trembling here, a feather.

The gentle artfulness of your restraint is what, of course, I love;
the gentleness that as I sit beside you
I can almost hold but can't, can't prove—

just like the look you give which, though I see,
I must refuse to catch and hold, as I imagine you'd
hold me.

But my hands, beside yours in the sunlight, can't refrain
from singing as I hold them in my lap;
and then a thousand birds begin to rise.

They sing and fly in the singing light
and the room is suddenly full of their music.
And I do not care that they will not listen.

And I do not care that they will not stop.

from *Poetry London*

Honeymoon

◇　◇　◇

Married—just—by the Caesar's Palace Bodhisattva,
my crown of flowers was flaking
and your pashmina grubbed the pavement
like torn toilet paper. "This means we'll be rich,"
you said, "and raise a set of sensitive sons."

I cried when the clerk at Arabian Nights
jimmied open a locker of letters, sent by my parents.
My parents were dead, or maybe abroad,
AWOL either way. I must have forgotten
I didn't know you that well.

I folded a cheque in my wallet
in place of a photo. The dude tambourined his keys
on his hip. "We'll take the top floor," I said.
"The highest," you said, blowing smoke to your left.
I knew you approved.

"This means we'll outlive our peers,
die amused and alone in the Hollywood Hills."
The elevator opened on Persia.
Carpets and mirrors were eating each other.
A vase sprouted white lilies,

"Symbolising marriage and death," you said.
The ornament of an asp
biting through its own neck
was anyone's guess, but right then
an obscure source of comfort.

from *Ambit*

Orpheus

◇   ◇   ◇

I

After I'd hustled, somehow, my way through overdrafts and overtime,
    goat-sitting,
busking on street corners—I drew quite a crowd—into the
    trans-continental-ticket bracket,
packed my handbooks and mosquito nets, boarded at the Styx and sung the
    long
ripped song of the aeroplane, a birdcall lost in chasing cloud, I landed
    slap-bang in the middle

of *Mahebourg Market, Mauritius*: the place I'd hoped to seek her out: my other
    half,
my home; the wandering, trapped part of my soul I'd been promised I could
    always return to.
I staggered when I got there though, under the weight of clatter and the
    strange stray dogs,
and white wolves of waves stroking the surfaces of a landscape burnt too hot
    for me.

And I despaired, the thing that I most wanted nowhere to be found
among the t-shirts imported from Japan, the clack of boules, the bang of
    stacked chapatti pans,
and behind the stalls, the gasps of local magicians astonished at themselves
and all they had to offer. Was that her eye in the eye of a fat round fish

flapping at the top of a silvery pile, sounding the echo of a sunbeam?
Was that her body turning in the pink jewelled sari held up for admiration,
moving like mobile hair or flayed skin? The imam called over my head,
remember to submit. The church bells told me, *come back to God*. Salt scent
    whispered

behind lashes and fingernails, weaving across the veins at my wrists. My
	lute bumped
against the suddenly wrong skin of my thigh, a skin too pale and too
	loosely held to bone,
as I dodged from toe to toe and string to string around the docks, never
	fast enough
to catch a single sincere note; as policemen with their bushed
	moustaches,

their blue shirts and shaded eyes watched me like deaf spirits, separated
	tourists
I saw who dared to kiss. Is this, sir, what you're looking for? Peek
	quickly or
they'll kick me out, he opened up the long flat hook of his grey
	suitcase, the lid swung up
like the stone before a tomb . . .

II

Many words have been offered to or given me:
*Greek or Turkish? Italiano, Espagnol? There's no way
you're not Israeli* or *Where was your mother from?*
At most, *You have the island look. Caribbean?*
but here they speak to me in Kreol, watch me

as I walk down the street—until I answer and,
as always, disappoint; my staccato English
failed again. So my mouth stays folded up.
I watch my grandparents instead
as they lie on tender beaches, remembering;

or else I watch the people as they move
from one small spot to the next. Their faces
are heavy in the shade, reflecting,
like thick glass tilted towards the sun,
nothing but the island's hot light. Nothing of me.

III

It's not many human creatures who—with skin
living and flexible working over solid limbs
full of dry, shining, salted bone,
a purple pumping heart, kidneys and lungs—
will know the feeling of complete immersion,
a journey to another land behind a wall of salt
and glass and water. It's not many who cross
that floating river, spitting pomegranate seeds,
and live to tell the tale.

But when you dove off that ledge or throne of rock
and felt the water popping in your ears,·
scouring your throat to take what it discovered there,
peeling that last layer of skin around your lips,
you knew you had become mankind, and knew
what you had found—a story that would save us all,
the hint of an ending in eighteen feet of water,
a glimpse of Eurydice.

And then the tight space in your chest denied
further investigation, the last page. You swam,
your eyes stinging too freely to look back,
the frog-kicks of your legs making their own
ripples, you stood a wet mess on the slippery surface,
your body newly yours, the laughing children
emerging from the dawn around you
to jump again and again
without a second thought.

from *Iota*

The Year Strikes the Rock

◊ ◊ ◊

The year strikes the rock
with one spoilt-child glance, like Athene,

the world's first olive tree
springs up, millions will follow,

their rough grey bark like lions' tongues,
their little squab branches

striving for sky at the year's command,
ankle-deep in poor thin dry soil.

The year is sleepless on her mother's side,
wants to live where a lake

lies quietly under the spell of its own name,
where evening makes a quiet copy of everything,

the year wants to live in
a leaky green caravan in Cadiz

or in an attic some place
where the world won't think of looking for her . . .

The year makes many an arduous journey,
one day scaling a mountain range,

the next scanning a flat mirage-ridden
monotony of sea ice,

now the year wears bird-feather gloves,
bluethroat, greenwing teal, swan of the tundra,

her sealskin boots are lined with caribou fur,
her cape sewn from the pelt of the Arctic hare . . .

At night, in the tent,
by the faint shine of the lamp,
the year carves maps on tablets of walrus ivory . . .

Poor year, her maps are out of date before the dawn . . .
So what?

She knows her work is never done,
she's a realist,

tucks all her weathers
under her humble hairy marvellous armpit,

just watch her making sunshine
from the gold of Frau Luther's wedding ring.

from *Ink Sweat and Tears*

Mustard

◊ ◊ ◊

Its flavour in the nostrils a thundercloud smart
like seeing your crush on a superstud's arm;
you'd have to be sturdier than durmast
oak to contain such a bastard stum
in your head's barrel and not cry out drams
of tears. But if you, in your dilemma, durst
eat another spoonful, your throat's drum
is often only half as stung, your heart's mud
stirred to a soup and every untoward smut
on your tongue expunged in one broad strum,
leaving nothing—no points, no clear datums
from which to measure pain, no lukewarm dust
of hurt feelings, rags clinging to an absurd mast
or pins or crumbs or flakes of seed-hard must.

from *Magma*

Communiqué

◇   ◇   ◇

Tiny-eared, tiny-fingered one,
the moon is there for you to visit,
the hotels at the bottom of the sea.

You will learn to savour Antrim wine
while eating deep-fried, nettle-wrapped
jellyfish on baked dock leaves.

Ah, the music that you'll listen to,
while levitating in the garden, the art
you'll see floating in the sky.

Ambassadors from other planets
will grace your phone tv screen,
with no translation needed. No,

language-barriers will be blasted,
the dog will confess to you
that he bit the travelling chef.

The email chip in your brain
will receive messages from the dead,
and will even answer them.

So this is a first communiqué,
one sent early. Take your time,
tiny one, but do respond to me.

from *The Dark Horse*

Some Sayings about the Snake

◊ ◊ ◊

after Helen Rousseau

The snake is imaginary, even in life.

We know it from a ribbon by its windings.

We know it by its movement, eyes, and fangs.

We know it from the apprehension we feel dreaming of it.

The snake arrives at dawn with the first light.

It enters through the ear and exits through the navel.

It coils itself within the gut and heart.

The snake is the primal scream in the grass.

It coils around the limbs of man and tree.

It lives under a stone in the guilty conscience.

It is necklace and armlet and bangle and song.

The snake is the air in a hollow tube.

The snake measures time the way man measures cloth.

The snake spells out its name in the sand.

The snake lives at the edges of life.

When the snake enters a book, the book closes.

from *Ambit*

Scart Gap

◇　◇　◇

I tuck in my dorsal spine in an attempt at lift.
We are watching for flying fish and his hand is on the helm and
lightly (as if a concertina of butterflies) we are beginning a process
towards which I have stretched long as the Milky Way.

Black dance-lettering, soft scarlet guelder berries, mull-white
are the birch, the barn owl, my hollow, inlet, hope, such as life is
in its un-filthiness tucked into the hem of a skirt whilst I hanker
after the want of the moon the muck of a hare.

Who are the mystics? At what incline a meeting-slope?
How will I steer amongst the sonic booms, the hunger,
the unhinged cranes? Will there be plenty of his manifold blessings?
Such things I dreamt and also the creaking of wings.

Moon as 'her' (why not), moss, a pilgrim's canvas bag, Venus
beglamoured in the southwest, a region of sedge-beds and waded fog
sweeping in with buddleia-tinted wing plates. A siren. Its belling
covering our hearts. Ten times our weight in water. Our father.

Who art a gull shrieks over the beet fields *who art who art*
Monos. Alone. That place.
Snowstorms trashing the horizon.
Alone. Tender cradle of bone.

from *Obsessed With Pipework*

103

The Long Horizon

◇ ◇ ◇

When all has been said and done and what remains is submergence
our bookshelves mulched and cathode ray tubes cracked under pressure

and a coelacanth noses our skulls on the carpet as it gums the last fibres,
the freezer aclick with live crabs and the windows gone back into sand,

as an octopus wraps itself around the steering wheel of our van
and thrusts out great billows of rust where the light fathoms slowly

over a copse of dead oaks given up to the brown limbs of algae,
and the horse in its trap is hollowed by seahorses into an ornament

having waited too long for an ark, and dust rolls through radio silence
reflected from satellites forever in orbit with no landing signal

and the waves have nowhere to crash except for the odd mountain steeple
where the last nesting gulls batter and fry as the lightning grounds

and there are no more words for rain when the only recognisable sound
is the sounding of bells slower than whalesong as the tides keep rising

with floating canopies of corpses that give up their gas and then sink
past the curious mouths of fish on the long drop back to the cities

and the leviathan rolls in Hyde Park beneath a waterlogged sky
and jellyfish parachute over Tokyo in the wartime flash of an eel,

tell me whose fingers will indent our daughter's ribs as her heels
dance the mad dance of the Jesus Christ lizard, hurdling the troughs

and the waves in the settling night, down onto her ramshackle cot with two handfuls of sushi? Who will praise her diligence?

from *The London Magazine*

Hasard

◇　◇　◇

Think *Taraxacum officinale*—a dandelion clock—
just that, and not
the idyll:
the product of focus groups, sanitized ads.

Please, forget the infants, their still-taut mothers,
the hyper-green grass.
And, if you can't
abstract a singular, globular head of seeds

—a greyish, Baudelairean candyfloss—
make the background
a patchy scrubland
or better still, a fissure of concrete.

And so . . . And so a halitosis wind kicks up
and sets off
each germ
upon its path. You lack the intellect, so

let's call such combinatorics
chance.
And let's
forget Coriolis, the geostrophic balance;

let us recall only the *lits hasardeux*
—those beds of chance—
in which
we have landed, taken root, read

'hazard, from *al-zahr* (the die), or *yasara* (he played at dice)'.

from *Magma*

Sheep

◊ ◊ ◊

for @dogsdoingthings

Sheep wearing short pink diner uniforms, serving coffee, startling easily.

Sheep being followed through evening streets, sensing danger, flocking
helplessly.

Sheep afraid in the nightclub chaos, hooves on the table, staring
blankly.

Sheep in the jaws of persistent death, hearing *come with me if you want to
live.*

Sheep on the run being told of the lamb that's yet to be born, the
essential future.

Sheep hysterical, laughing, incredulous. Domestic sheep who can't
balance a chequebook.

Sheep being taught to make household bombs, to fire guns, weave steel
wool.

Sheep growing up on a motel bed. Sheep counting sheep, making love
before dawn.

Sheep being found, corralled, being hounded. Sheep firing shots from a
speeding car.

Sheep being blown from the tank's explosion, fighting metal with flesh,
nearing exhaustion.

Sheep left nosing their lover's limp body. Sheep pulling themselves up.
Sheep finishing it.

Sheep driving with a shotgun on the empty seat, their own dogs for
protection, as the new life kicks.

from *Rising*

Table Manners

◊ ◊ ◊

Let's have you sitting straight. Your relationship with
furniture comes first. Don't be marooned
at the linen's edge: etiquette's a dialect
to help. Hold your napkin like an injured bird

then unfurl its water lily to quilt your lap.
Keep a candle to the centre of the map,
gerbera to your right, unless, that is, you've
anything to hide, in which case,

make it two. Do not remove your shoes or
show any flesh. Tilt your soup's light towards
her, like an invitation to swim. Sip
as though you're working on it. Elbows off!

If she asks for salt, remember pepper's
spoken for. Don't stare. Set your smile to
simmer. Stand when a lady leaves. If you catch
yourself distorted in a fork, do not fret

with the cruet or a match; we don't leave marks
except on glass. Cutlery is a code: if your
implements kiss on the plate this indicates
you're after more. Ten to five means it's over.

from *New Welsh Review*

MICHAEL ZAND

on a persian cairn

◇   ◇   ◇

a bride shivers . in the sebber air
rawthey . leaf-fringed . tiptoed

but we turn . beauty at our backs
grinding . spinning through . faded

working the stones . shaping at dusk
the line of the sunset drips . chipping

een mey . mara khahad bord
omar is with me now . his lovely rats

tap . mouthing your name . for forough
and again . the mason thwats . and ats

an audience of strays . many young birds
beneath the trees . a spell circles them

and the hits . now to the time of a duduk
cannot fade as the rest do . hollow

all lengths are panting . cloyed . burning
the old man stut ters . emshab miravim

tonight . float them . off shore wind
down the long street . exhausted and dirty

a passer by . by an uninvited language
is tehran . without the need for monoliths

words are related to this but not the same
their lives are stubborn . strong . tractable

unequal in demand . frightening
crumbling in tigris and lune . reeded

and when we stock . the fear stops
simple pretexts . palms of our hands

when a deed is worth a word . we smile
a sting of memory . the green in her eyes

when a dipthong stops . carries a gun
a poem is a taxi in a sandstorm . flayling

narcissus becomes a flower of burden
a lit cigarette . a mild tap . a brigg echo

in this beautiful decay . they plant it . right
at zahira dowleh . it still chisels . full of frap

and all of us are now a whole . sacrifice
to whispers and twitters . inner prancing

from *ninerrors Freak Lung*

CONTRIBUTORS' NOTES AND COMMENTS

GILLIAN ALLNUTT has published seven collections of poetry. The most recent is *How the Bicycle Shone: New & Selected Poems* (Bloodaxe, 2007). *Nantucket and the Angel* and *Lintel* were both shortlisted for the T.S. Eliot Prize and *Lintel* was a Poetry Book Society Choice. In 2005 she won the Northern Rock Foundation Writer's Award. She lives in Co. Durham. Of 'in her kitchen', she writes, "In the summer of 2007 I accompanied a friend to some of a series of chemotherapy treatments she was then undergoing as an outpatient in a Newcastle hospital. On a lovely day in July we escaped unexpectedly early from one of these and drove to the coast at Seaton Sluice and walked a bit. The path led past a big striped circus tent in a field, waiting on its own for the evening show. There was something so cheerful and forlorn about it. My friend had a vase of delphiniums on the kitchen table and the poem began next morning as I waited for her to wake. It gave me up to blue. I am hugely grateful for the existence and work of the NHS, but I incline towards a more holistic approach than the one it takes to the healing of human beings. There is an area of deep disquiet around this in me and it reflects itself in the poem."

MIKE BANNISTER, author of *Greenstreet Fragments* (Orphean Press, 2003) and of *Pocahontas in Ludgate* (Arrowhead Press, 2007) was nominated for The Housman Society's Poetry Prize in 1992 and was winner of the 2009 George Crabbe Memorial Poetry Competition. His poems have appeared in *The London Magazine*, *Other Poetry*, *Brittle Star* and *The Long Poem Magazine*. Mike lives in Halesworth, Suffolk, where he is Chair of *Café Poets*, a bi-monthly venue for working poets across the region. He is presently at work on his third collection *The Weir of Orinsay*. Mike writes, "I feel that Wordsworth gets closest to it, in his *Preface to Lyrical Ballads (1802.)* He talks about 'chusing' incidents from common life; so as to describe them in plain words, over which is thrown '*a certain colouring of imagination*'. 'Satin Moth' could be read like that, as some kind of affirmation of the value we place on maintaining our relationship with the natural world. It is one thing to venture outdoors, to feel with all five senses, the reality of being alive, but when Nature's own ambassador comes to call, it is a privilege of quite another order. Some may detect, in 'Satin Moth', the 'birthing' of a poem; as *The Preface* has it '*the manner in which we associate ideas in a state of excitement*'. The poet, having conducted his 'ambassador' safely into the night, lies wondering why the incident stirred him so, and how he might recapture the moment. As poet's do, he examines the event through a multiple lens, of history, learning, memory, belief, close observation and wonder, before attempting to make his experience memorable. In resolution, he re-presents, with just a hint of travelling showmanship, (or is it Bardic hwyl?) the exquisite spectacle of that nighttime visitation."

CHRIS BECKETT grew up in Ethiopia in the 1960's. His poems have appeared in magazines including *Poetry London*, *Smiths Knoll* and *Wasafiri*. He won the *Poetry London* competition in 2001 and second prize in Chroma 2006. His second collection *Ethiopia Boy* will be published by Carcanet Oxford Poets in 2013. He has also translated work by the young Ethiopian poet and novelist, Bewketu Seyoum for *Modern Poetry in Translation*. Of his poem, he writes, "the boast is an African self-praise poem, particularly associated with warriors and coming-of-age ceremonies for boys. It is normally a list of kills or fine deeds that the boaster is proud of and wants his listeners to fear or admire. My poem grew out of a recent trip back to Ethiopia where I lived as a boy, during which I found out that my best friend Abebe had died. One day I picked up a fly-whisk and it seemed to spring to life in my defence! Just the feel of it took me back to my boyhood, the flicky hairy itchiness of it all . . .even the sound of the word *whisk* is simultaneously soft but cutting (that final *k*). As I sat there trying to deal with my own flies of memory and grief, it was as if the old whisk was shouting his boast in my hand."

EMILY BERRY was an Eric Gregory Award winner in 2008, and her pamphlet *Stingray Fevers* was published by Tall Lighthouse the same year. Her poems have been widely published, including in the Bloodaxe anthology *Voice Recognition: 21 Poets for the 21st Century* (2009). She is a co-writer (with four others) of *The Breakfast Bible*, a compendium of breakfasts to be published by Bloomsbury in 2012. She lives in London, where she was born. She writes, "I often find it difficult to comment on my poems. I think it's partly a reluctance to elaborate, since I hope they would speak for themselves, and I worry that anything I would add might limit or diminish them in some way. I suppose, like many of my poems, this one began as a sort of dramatisation of my own emotions, but the final narrative is very far removed from the starting point and has become an independent story. Some time after I'd written the poem it made me think of a horrible book I used to be obsessed with when I was a teenager— *Flowers in the Attic* by Virginia Andrews, sort of seventies American gothic in which four siblings are locked in an attic by their evil grandmother. I think that might have influenced the poem on some level—not in terms of the narrative exactly, but atmospherically maybe. I don't really know who the characters in the poem are, or where they came from, but I'm very scared of Arlene! She has appeared in a poem I've written since and I think she may be quite a tough demon to exorcise."

LIZ BERRY was born in the Black Country and now lives in London where she works as an infant school teacher. She received an Eric Gregory Award in 2009. Her debut pamphlet The Patron Saint of Schoolgirls was published by tall-lighthouse in 2010. She is Emerging Poet in Residence at Kingston University and a 2011 Arvon/Jerwood mentee. She writes, "'The Year We Married Birds' was inspired by a kingfisher I watched one afternoon as I was walking along the canal in Wolverhampton. It struck me how gorgeous and fascinating we find birds, while they have little to no interest in us. I thought of friends of mine in love with unobtainable men and how easily our longing and imagination allow us to hitch our hopes and fantasies onto almost any creature or situation. I wanted the poem to be romantic and playful, surreal but at the same time believable. Many of the birds in the poem are only doing what birds normally do — migrating, hovering, nesting on cliffs — while the young women, including the narrator, sweep themselves off into a world of winged romance."

NINA BOYD lives in Huddersfield. She is an active member of a thriving poetry community in West Yorkshire, is particularly interested in the Edwardian period and is now dabbling in fiction, as well as continuing to write innumerable poems about mad women and sad children. She was the overall winner of the 2009 Poetry Business Book and Pamphlet Competition. Her first collection, Dear Mr Asquith, was published by Smith/Doorstop Books in 2010. She has a Postgraduate Diploma in Creative Writing, with Distinction, from Manchester Metropolitan University. She writes, "I wrote 'Lanterns' on a car journey. Seeing a horse and foal in a field, I noticed the way the foal's legs splayed like the legs of a trestle table, so that it looked unstable and ungainly, leaning against the mare. I am touched by the way horses, like people, lean into one another for support.

Much of my writing is about strange human behaviour, and at the time, I was fascinated by the idea of people who disappear without any warning, and the exhilaration they might feel at letting go and leaving everything behind. I thought of a gentle person, closer to animals than to other people, who doesn't fit in to the world of men, and longs for escape. This poem is the nearest I get to creating a landscape painting. I have no abilities with pencil or brush; but words paint pictures too, and the reader can fill in the background for himself. I like the idea of poems as starting points for the reader, who can make of them whatever his imagination cares to see. I was conscious of the need for colour in the poem (violet, orange); and both movement (leans, fans strokes, flicks, staggering, drift) and the contrasting tethering of the last line."

JAMES BROOKES was born in 1986 and grew up in rural Sussex. He read English and Creative Writing at the University of Warwick and then studied at the College of Law, Guildford. He is now the Williams Librarian at Cranleigh School in Surrey where he also teaches English and History. In 2009 he received an Eric Gregory Award from the Society of Authors; his pamphlet *The English Sweats* was published by Pighog Press in the same year. He was awarded a Hawthornden Fellowship in 2011. His first full collection is forthcoming from Salt Publishing in 2012. He comments, "I should first admit that I've never been to Kaliningrad, chief city of that strange oblast of land that was once East Prussia, annexed to Russia after the Potsdam Conference of 1945 when just a little while before, ancient Konigsberg (as it was then) had been looted and levelled by the tides of war.

I do however own a Soviet medal for the capture of Koenigsburg, sold cheap to me by a street dealer in Moscow as a souvenir; this yellow ed bit of tat was my initial prompt. As to the whereabouts of the panels of amber that once decorated the fabled room, I have no idea—whether they w131ere seized by Soviet forces, spirited away by fleeing Nazis or simply destroyed along with much of the old town is a teaser for conspiracy theorists. Given the city's experience of Communism I did have Marx on my mind when choosing a title, though I'm more inclined towards Bill Bailey's adage: 'opiates are the opiates of the people.' Human rapacity—for material wealth, for intoxication, for anything transverbera-tive—seems pretty broad in its tastes. Though I don't wish to libel a place I have never visited, since the early nineties Kaliningrad has seen (poor Marx!) an explosion of free enterprise in the heroin trade.

Nonetheless the poem was never intended as a history, geography or politics lesson; in its earliest stages it existed as part of a short sequence of 'Variations on a Theme of Gold'. I was trying to see how widely I could range—in terms of vocabulary and historical material—whilst in a limited palate of colour and a particular location. But the marginality and the mad contrasts of Kaliningrad/Konigsberg carry this amazing sense of displace-ment; I've tried to capture that impression. If the poem is about any one thing then it is about the problem of what we choose to treasure and what we hope to gain and risk to loose by doing so."

JUDY BROWN was born in Cheshire and now divides her time between London and Derbyshire. Her first full collection is *Loudness* (Seren, 2011). A pamphlet *Pillars of Salt* (2006) was a winner of Templar Poetry's pamphlet competition. She won the Manchester Poetry Prize in 2010 and the Poetry London Competition in 2009. Of 'The Helicopter Visions', Brown writes, "early morning and late at night police helicopters fly low over South London. You hear them but you never seem to see them. It's a frightening sound. And I was interested in writing about jobs and lives in which isolation comes with the turf. I liked aerial views of London too. When my family sat with my stepfather in St Christopher's Hospice through the last day and evening, there were Saturday papers which grew ragged as we handed them round. In one there was an interview with the pilot of one of these helicopters. Everything was left behind when the day ended. When I came to write the poem a few months later, I couldn't remember much about the article apart from two vague observations: that it is tricky to navigate across a city and that the helicopter's instruments are highly sensitive. Something of that day, and the painful transitions between states which it involved, might have come to fill the gap left in the story. It took four years to get the poem to feel right."

MARK BURNHOPE was born in 1982 and currently lives and writes in Bournemouth, Dorset. He studied at London School of Theology before completing a Creative Writing MA at Brunel University. His poems and reviews have appeared in print and online magazines including *Magma*, *Nth Position*, *Ink Sweat & Tears*, *Horizon Review*, *Eyewear* and *Stride*. His debut pamphlet, *The Snowboy*, is available from Salt Publishing. He writes, "I enjoy many of the big dead poets who dealt with big, dead subjects, like despair: Auden, Tennyson, Dickinson, Plath. I think we ignore them at our peril. But people can be cynical, so we have to keep finding new strategies for dealing with old themes. This title (the whole poem, really) is partly tongue-in-cheek. A play on twelve-step addiction programmes, it doesn't let on what 'better despair' might be: despair which is more expe-rienced / profound / intelligent / creative/ cool? I'm not sure. Having Spina bifida, I find it interesting that in this therapeutic context, the word 'step' is stripped of any association with physicality: to take a step is to improve. How did language 'arrive' at this? Anyway, I envisaged a kind of instruc-tion manual for the amateur and professional despair junkie, which churns up poetic and self-help language, making fun of the inadequacies in both.

Most of the imagery and ideas are borrowed from the landscape around Bournemouth: age-old, but with a chic white perfection, as if it's been cleaned for the tourists. Even the cliffs gleam like plastic garden furniture. Bournemouth town has an odd reputation as a "retirement village" full of teenage yobs (an unlikely paradox if I ever heard one). In this poem too, youth and age seemed to want to play tug-of-war, have a bar fight. If they agree on anything at all, it's that Time has little patience with machismo. It doesn't care what boat you buy, only that you take it for a spin while you can."

KAYO CHINGONYI was born in Zambia in 1987 and came to the UK in 1993. He studied English Literature at The University of Sheffield where he co-founded a poetry night called 'Word Life'. His poems are published in *City Lighthouse* (tall-lighthouse, 2009), *The Shuffle Anthology* (Shuffle Press, 2009), *Verbalized* (British Council, 2010), *Paradise by Night* (Booth-Clibborn Editions, 2010), *Clinic II* (Egg Box Publishing, 2011) and *The Salt Book of Younger Poets* (Salt Publishing, 2011). He is a visiting writer at Kingston University. He writes of 'Andrew's Corner': "I originally wrote a slightly different version of this poem for an event celebrating Bob Dylan's 'Subterranean Homesick Blues' back in 2009. I was given a line from the song to use as a starting point: 'the pumps don't work because the vandals took the handles'. This got me thinking about filling stations which in turn suggested a particular filling station close to a junction I know very well. With this in mind, I started writing and 'Andrew's Corner' is what emerged. After a reading I gave recently, which included this poem, I was asked by an audience member if I had intended it to be a social commentary to which I replied that I hadn't and that I very rarely write poems with that conscious intention. I think of this poem as a sketch rather than a photograph and it was probably this idea of sketching that prompted me to write it in three short sections made up of lists of images. There isn't much else to say except that this poem was written, as many of my poems are, in the early hours of the morning which might account for the tone of the last section."

JANE COMMANE is a poet, tutor and co-editor of Nine Arches Press and *Under the Radar* magazine. She was born in Coventry in 1983 and lives and works in Warwickshire. Her poems have been published in *Horizon Review, Gists and Piths, Litter, Hand + Star* and *Tears in the Fence*. Of 'Music', she writes the following, "This poem comes from a recent sequence called 'Lessons from *The School of Rock*'. I wanted this sequence to imagine an alternative curriculum, the one I had in my mind and my imagination when I was growing up, whilst simultaneously revisiting that time in my life, at school in the midlands town where I still live. I had always been surrounded by a huge range of music throughout childhood, and in the mid-to-late nineties, as I became a teenager, it suddenly became absolutely vital to me, a powerful catalyst and source of inspiration that fired some of my early writings. I was the kind of person at school who stayed in the library at lunchtimes reading the *NME* or *Melody Maker*, and this poem is intended as an anthem of sorts for those who never quite fitted in at school. Music was one thing (alongside books) that kept me going as a teenager, so in a way this poem is also about both escapism and trying to be heard, and the joint powers of poetry and music to do this."

FRED D'AGUIAR is the author of eleven books of poetry and fiction which have been translated into a dozen languages, and a number of essays, one of which was included in *Best American Essays* 2000. His play *A Jamaican Airman Foresees His Death* (produced at Royal Court Theatre Upstairs in 1991, and published by Methuen, London in 1995). His BBC-commissioned radio play, *Days and Nights in Bedlam,* was broadcast and webcast in October 2005. His most recent book, Continental Shelf (Carcanet, 2009) was a U.K. Poetry Book Society Choice and shortlisted for the UK's T.S. Eliot Prize 2009. Born in London of Guyanese parents and brought up in Guyana, he teaches creative writing at Virginia Tech. He relates the following, "I happened to be in Toulouse and heard about the mythic rose of the place. I met a lot of people along the way and from a combination of our talk and my thoughts about what I observed I happened upon this poem. You can see me taking the temperature of a black diaspora presence in Europe (in this case, Toulouse, Paris, Montpelier) and balancing those ideas with some autobiographical and artistic concerns. I enjoy reading (and writing) poems that work with all three areas: place, time, and, the body."

EMMA DANES has worked as a writer, editor, teacher and web researcher. She has won the Hamish Canham Prize (with '17') and the Poetry Society Stanza Poetry Competition, and also been runner up in both competitions in other years. She was shortlisted in the tall-lighthouse pamphlet competition, and commended in the Troubadour Poetry Prize. Her poems have been published in *Poetry Wales, Poetry News, The North* and *Magma,* and in the Templar anthology *Buzz.* She lives with her family in Ely. She writes, "I wrote '17' after I moved with my family from London to Cambridgeshire. I was apprehensive about the move, having lived in London all my life. We'd bought our first house there, intending to stay for many years. It was an old property which demanded constant work, and yet despite all our care and attention, it never quite seemed to belong to us. Years later it remains a strong, rather haunting presence in my mind.

I had been thinking of writing about the house for a while, and finally got down to it when 'home' was set as the theme for a *Poetry News* competition. The shape of the poem determined itself quite quickly. The regular line lengths, supported by internal rhyme and assonance, formed a house-like structure, to counterbalance the shifting undercurrents of mood and imagery. The poem falls into two halves—the first two stanzas describe our attempts to co-exist with the house; in the last two we escape from each other.

The poem surprised me with its rather melancholy, mysterious atmosphere. Jane Yeh described it as a 'submerged narrative of loss and mourning.' I did love our old house, but I think sometimes poems come from the more marginal or suppressed feelings we have. They are aspects of the truth which it would be difficult to express in any other way."

AMY DE'ATH was born in Suffolk in 1985. She studied at the University of East Anglia and in Philadelphia, US, before moving to Australia and then London. Her publications include *Erec & Enide* (Salt, 2010), and *Andromeda / The World Works for Me* (Crater Press, 2010). She has a new chapbook, *Caribou*, due out soon from Grasp Press. Her writing has appeared or is forthcoming in *Open Letter: a Canadian Journal of Writing and Theory*, *Jacket2*, *Esque*, *QUID*, *onedit*, and *Vlak* magazine. She lives and works in London, and is currently Poet in Residence at the University of Surrey. In September 2011 she will begin a PhD at Simon Fraser University in Vancouver, Canada. She writes, "Poetry has the capacity to be everything at once; and a poet's task—for me at least—is not to provide an accurate representation of life, or 'things as they are'; but to write in order to move thought, imagine new ways of existing, render the impossible possible. I believe the best way to do this is to write outside of conventional logic, and into a *precise disorder*; a considered form of non-sense. In a time of spoon-fed ideologies and homogenising systems, perhaps poetry can be an antidote to the effects of our alienation from our own bodies or our isolation within the world at large. In the words of Gertrude Stein, 'if you enjoy a thing you understand it'. So here's an unanswerable song, 'Lena at the Beach'."

ISOBEL DIXON was born in South Africa, where her prize-winning debut *Weather Eye* (Carapace, 2001) was published. Her poems have appeared in journals like *The Paris Review*, *The Guardian,* and *Magma*, and anthologies like *New Writing*, Penguin's *Poems for Love* and *The Forward Book of Poetry*. She was shortlisted for the Strokestown Poetry Prize 2011 and has been involved in several multi-poet events, including *Psycho Poetica*. Her recent collections, both from Salt in the UK, are *A Fold in the Map* (2007) and *The Tempest Prognosticator* (2011), described by J.M. Coetzee as 'a virtuoso collection'. She lives in Cambridge.

She says, "My Mississippi poet friend Benjamin Morris hosted a convivial poetry workshop group while finishing his PhD in Cambridge, and I went along a couple of times. As well as being a fine poet, he is also a cocktail aficionado of note, an enthusiastic mixologist with a gift for the creative naming of various original and exotic concoctions. I'm a regular classic cocktail kind of girl, nothing outrageous, but it was Ben's naming a particular drink 'Cloud Atlas' that kicked this poem off. I couldn't remember the recipe (though suspected, knowing Ben, that bourbon probably featured*), but know that the poem's initial ingredients were its first three lines.

These words were brewing in my head as I sat at my desk, and the rest of the cocktail titles were all waiting on the spines of the volumes on my study bookshelf. The poem somehow poured itself out, as some poems do: Jan Morris's *Trieste and the Meaning of Nowhere*, Ovid's *Metamorphoses*, Alain Corbin's *The Lure of the Sea*, W.G. Sebald's *Rings of Saturn*, Dante and some travel books, all alchemised into imaginary potions of seduction. But beyond the name game and the original inspiration of David Mitchell's novel on the cocktail maker, the poem is a fiction, a complete concoction, its characters bearing no resemblance to any persons known to me . . ."

*And Ben has kindly confirmed this suspicion and let us in on the secret:

Cloud Atlas

    1.5 oz bourbon (Bulleit or Woodford Reserve)
    1.5 oz pineapple juice
    1 tsp Galliano
    Lemon peel garnish (optional)

Shake bourbon and pineapple juice together with ice in a cocktail shaker. Let settle, and strain liquid only into a chilled martini glass. Open the shaker and add the Galliano to the emulsified foam, and mix thoroughly. Spoon mixture over the top of the drink, and dust with a pinch of cinnamon or nutmeg to finish. This drink is ideal for wintertime or any time. Best served with friends.

SASHA DUGDALE is a poet and translator. Her collections include *Notebook* (2003), *The Estate* (2007) and *Red House* (2011), all published by Carcanet / Oxford Poets. Her translations of the Russian poet Elena Shvarts *Birdsong on the Seabed* were a PBS recommended translation and shortlisted for the Popescu and Rossica Prizes. She also translates Russian plays for theatre, and she has worked for the Royal Court, the BBC, the RSC and the Tricycle.

She writes: "'Shepherds' is a poem about the South Downs. For most of my life I have lived a little more than a mile away from the Downs, but this is one of the first poems I have ever written about them. I walk on the Downs for hours every week and although there are flocks of sheep grazing all over the Downs there are no longer any shepherds. The Sussex shepherds were famous for their distinctive dress and habits. They often lived in little wagons, towed by horses to a place on the hills where they could oversee their flock and sleep in solitude. They carried crooks and wore smocks and tall hats and in the evening they read their Bibles. They were often buried with a clutch of wool on their breast to show God the reason for their absence from the little churches at the foot of the Downs. In this poem I also mention saints with withy ropes. This is a reference to a local 7th century saint called Cuthbert, who carried his mother in a wheelbarrow with withy (or willow stem) ropes about his neck. In the place where the barrow fell apart, Steyning, he built a church. I am always moved by the sight of the Downs from below. They look almost implausible—a green tidal wave. The long easy back of the Downs is mostly deserted when I walk, and sometimes quite still and haunted. This poem is an elegy for the last dwellers on the Downs, and a hymn of praise to the hills themselves."

IAN DUHIG has written six books of poetry, most recently *Pandorama* (Picador 2010). He has won the Forward Best Poem Prize once, the National Poetry Competition twice and three times been shortlisted for the T.S. Eliot Prize. He writes, "This is a companion piece to a poem called 'Jericho Shanty', which appears earlier in *Pandorama*, the collection title referring to Bert White's box of tricks in 'The Ragged-Trousered Philanthropists'. In both poems, 'Jericho' has no specific location but means, as in the *OED*, 'a place far distant and out of the way.' However, 'Jericho Shanty' revolves around the heroic achievements of the early railway-making navvies while this poem is about degeneration, attempting to imitate Sterne's narrative sidetracking of the Lockean trains of association in 'Tristram Shandy' but in a context of industrial entropy, also reflected by iambics which frequently break down into decasyllabics. A Proto Pipe is used for smoking cannabis, and to me at least resembles a miniature steam locomotive engine. Yorkshire suffers the highest instance of copper rail cable-theft in the UK, now of considerable scrap value. The cover of *Pandorama* is from an art box by Leeds surrealist Tony Earnshaw, appearing here, who would surely have been better-known if he'd lived in London. Born locally too, Alan Bennett has written of Auden nearly putting him off poetry by his views on where it should come from. Bennett appears as the poem's speaker is increasingly disjointed, claustrophobic and paranoid, but still uses Bennett's texts accurately. Finally, Leeds is the ur-goth city, as the BBC's recent 'Frankenstein' showed, set in the same Kirkstall Abbey mentioned in this poem."

JOSH EKROY lives in London. He was the winner of the Bedford Poetry Competition 2008, was commended in The Poetry London Competition 2009, and won third prize in the Keats-Shelley Memorial Prize 2009, among others. His poems have appeared in *The Rialto*, *Smith's Knoll*, *The SHOp*, *Other Poetry* and *Equinox*. He writes, "Trust the tale not the teller. I could say that by an odd coincidence I've recently been working on a poem called 'Love-Song of the Stylus' which perhaps atones for some of the damage done here through an attempt to write about the sexual relationship between the diamond stylus and vinyl. Imagine having a Mahler symphony transmitted through your body. You'd have to be a diamond to come out alive. I could say the reason for my writing on this theme is because I'm a frustrated musician. (But would that be true? Who knows?) It's certainly true I listen to classical music a lot but can play no instrument, although I have tried. Oh, how I've tried. But if I were to write directly about my frustrations with Grade One Piano, I don't think the result would be quite so interesting. Not to me, anyway, and I think 78 rpm is an attempt at a love-song too. Where's the romance or interest in a CD tray? Hm, come to think of it . . ."

LAURA ELLIOTT graduated from Norwich School of Art and Design in 2009 and subsequently won the Café Writers Norfolk Commission, which enabled her to travel to Serbia and complete her debut pamphlet collection *Bridge,* published by Gatehouse Press in 2010. She is currently completing a Masters in Creative Writing Poetry at the University of East Anglia, focusing on the relationship between written language and the visual arts. She notes that, " 'White Lace Nightgown' is a still life poem in which tensions between two people are expressed by the objects which surround them. The poem is domestic insofar as it seeks to draw attention to the subtle interiors of both the relationship and the situation itself, highlighting the fragility of love. Touch is a primary sensation within this room, establishing points of contact between the personal and objectifiable world. In this small space, brief images of the body punctuate the environment by way of items littered about the room, serving to articulate more about the disturbance affecting the characters than they are capable of themselves. An atmosphere of intimacy is therefore manifest in an otherwise silent composition, where the parts and pieces of the scene speak on behalf of the voiceless couple, unifying them as a whole. The end of the poem however is unsettling, the reader is left only with a lasting impression of unease between the couple, a feeling which has been present and intensified throughout."

American expatriate CARRIE ETTER has lived in England since 2001. Her first collection, *The Tethers* (Seren, 2009), won the London New Poetry Award, and her second, *Divining for Starters*, was published by Shearsman Books in 2011; she has also edited an anthology, *Infinite Difference: Other Poetries by UK Women Poets* (Shearsman, 2010). She is a senior lecturer in creative writing at Bath Spa University. Of her poem 'Prairie', she writes that it "records one of my favourite experiences when visiting my family home in Normal, Illinois: going to sleep and hearing a train's long whistle around one a.m. The mention of sleepers refers to Whitman's poem of that title, prescience to the intuition of dreams."

DAI GEORGE lives sometimes in London and sometimes in Cardiff. He writes about contemporary poetry in journals such as *Boston Review*, *Poetry Wales* and *Poetry Review*. His first collection is forthcoming from Seren in 2013. He comments, "As is often the case, the key to the meaning of this poem lies in a phrase I cut because it gave too much away. In what was once the fourth stanza, I looked askance at 'this generation of expensive taste and slender means' who expect the 'summer birthrights' of annual holidays somewhere nice in southern Europe.

I wrote the piece after having been on just such a holiday with my girlfriend and her parents last summer. We went to the south of France, to stay in a beautiful guesthouse owned by friends of the family. While there, I realised that I could enjoy a kept life as egregious as that of any low-rent member of the aristocracy, in a land that historically had taken a rather dim view of its landed classes. I know others in my so-called 'lost generation' who are in a similar position: we're miles off being able to afford this lifestyle ourselves, yet, through a combination of entitlement, complacency and a genuinely happy relationship with our parents' genera-tion, we continue to enjoy its luxuries and trappings.

On noticing this, a type of paranoia started to take hold. Chubby bees loping round the lavender turned into a threatening mob; the friendly Belgian gardener started to resemble Robespierre. Who knows how much longer an impoverished, ageing society will put up with us? Or how long before hungrier cultures—such as in India or Brazil—overtake us for good? I should take this opportunity to clarify that, though the poem expresses a complicated feeling, I have a rather more straightforward sense of gratitude and fondness towards the people and places it alludes to. I hope I'll be allowed back for more soul-searching, at any rate."

GILES GOODLAND was born in Taunton, was educated at the universities of Wales and California, took a D. Phil at Oxford, has published several books of poetry including *A Spy in the House of Years* (Leviathan, 2001) and *Capital* (Salt, 2006). He works in Oxford as a lexicographer and lives in West London. He has a new book forthcoming from Salt in 2012. He writes, "As often with my poems, this one came from a mixture of observation of the moment and a jumble of old notes. Staying at a beach chalet with the kids, I was playing with the idea that the humours in the eyeball have a similar composition to seawater, and I read somewhere that this is a relict from our very distant evolutionary past. We all carry a little bit of ocean with us, and use it to look with. This combined with being on a beach with my children and thinking about the various meanings of waves. Sound also is very important in the poem and I allowed myself to get carried away with some slightly outrageous sound-alike words and phrases (just as waves repeat themselves, each one slightly differently). Something about the sea always seems to loosen me up in my use of words (being away from work is a help, I suppose). So I let the words play around, as the children were doing, in my notebook. Language is like the sea, as a whole it is formless, but it can form localized shapes called sentences or even poems. The poem ends with the children, and that feeling of having the ground pulled under you when a wave rolls back into the surf. Sitting on the beach watching them, I got the idea for the poem: we are like waves, we carry sea with us, generation after generation. If that is not a misunderstanding, and even if it is, it is one I can run with."

MATTHEW GREGORY was born in Suffolk in 1984. He was educated at the Norwich School of Art and Design and Goldsmiths College. His work has appeared in *Poetry London*, *The Rialto*, *Magma*, the anthology series *Stop Sharpening Your Knives*, and has been aired on BBC Radio. In 2010, he received an Eric Gregory award. He writes, "There is a tradition of poems that give emotional agency to a wounded or vulnerable animal, in which the animal often appears as a gift or a burden shared between two people. With 'Young Pterodactyl', I tried to interrupt that tradition and estrange it from itself, introducing an 'agent' from somewhere outside the natural territory of both the poem and its tradition, in the hope that I might surprise something out of it. A kind of alchemy—the poet trying new substances and combinations in his pestle, here element X, in the form of the hatchling pterosaur is introduced to Y, suburban domesticity and Z, the mechanism of the poem. Ultimately, I think I intended to write something that was as uncertain and as unready to identify itself as the strange creature in the leaves."

PHILIP GROSS's collection *The Water Table* won the T.S. Eliot Prize 2009, while *I Spy Pinhole Eye*, with photographer Simon Denison, won Wales Book of the Year. A new collection *Deep Field*, dealing with aphasia, is due from Bloodaxe in November 2011. His books of children's poetry include *The All-Nite Café* which won the Signal Award, while *Off Road To Everywhere* won the CLPE Award for the best book of children's poetry published in 2010. He has published ten novels for young people, including *The Lastling*, and since 2004 has been Professor of Creative Writing at Glamorgan University, where he leads the M Phil in Writing programme.

He writes, "Looked at from one angle, this is a snapshot—one moment that literally happened, one chance of the light, the kind of thing that's gone before you can turn to the people you're with and say 'Look!' In this case they were small children, whose response might anyway have been 'So?' Though the 'so?' of it is what the poem is about, or what makes it a poem. Looked at from another angle, there have been wild-fowl passing thought my poems all my writing life, coming partly from earliest known art of my Finno-Ugrian ancestors (my father is Estonian) and more recently appearing in the mud-and-water-scapes of the Severn Estuary. I stared at that body of water throughout my book *The Water Table*, and what I found reflected and refracted in it was a whole series of questions about the boundaries of things. Is the estuary the border between countries, or an access to a wider world beyond? Is it a river or a sea? Are the mud banks that dissolve and reform the same thing, though they're different every day?

To say I found myself asking the same questions about the self, my own and my loved ones' selves, might sound academic, except that they arose from just looking, not from abstract thought. Most of all, they came from being alongside my elderly father as he lost his language (several languages) to aphasia and deafness, and increasingly also his memories and other habits that define us as ourselves. So the fact that I noticed this moment on a lake in Cosmeston Country Park while walking with grandchildren preoccupied with the business of learning the world and the language, becoming themselves, might not be accidental after all. Not that I planned it or intended it, but I was in some sense working on it. Both angles are true. The fact that they intersected there and then was a gift of the light."

KELLY GROVIER was educated at Oxford University, where he wrote his doctorate on the Romantic philosopher and poet 'Walking' Stewart (1747–1822). He is a regular contributor on arts to the *Times Literary Supplement* and co-founder of the scholarly journal *European Romantic Review*. He has written widely on the poetry of William Wordsworth and John Keats and is the author of The Gaol: the story of Newgate, London's most notorious prison. His first collection of poems, *A lens in the palm*, appeared in 2008 with Carcanet Press and a reading of his work is featured on the online Poetry Archive. He writes, "The poem stems from an actual sighting—the fleetingest of glimpses amid the crush of visitors entering the museum of what I could swear was a small blue butterfly clinging to the sleeve of a little girl, part of a school group with matching satchels—an art class, I supposed, on a sketching field trip. Suddenly, the trajectory of these improbable companions traced itself in my mind as they made their imagined way through the galleries. I liked the idea of their whizzing past a whole history of human devices designed to keep permeable the membrane between this world and the next: the funerary decorations of Egyptian scarab beetles, the alchemical paraphernalia of Queen Elizabeth I's conjurer, Dr Dee, and the fifteenth-century mosaic skull of the Mexican god, *Tezcatlipoca*, or 'Smoking Mirror'. Vaguely aware of classical notions attaching to butterflies as symbols of the soul, I wanted to play with the possibility that these two visitors were at once aspects of each other yet utterly separate, as though life and death were themselves complementary states—simultaneous, mirroring—rather than sequential.

That the child, with 'sketch book and pen', is herself a creator and the butterfly, her soul, a thing of artistic expression that loses itself in the reflections of the galleries' glass cases ('its hieroglyphs ghosting / into cartouched tombs'), allowed a blurring of the lines between life and artefact as well as between life and death. The fancy that the iridescent wings would eventually, amid a frenzy of smartphone camera flashes, dissolve upwards past the geometry of the building's skylight was intended to introduce a final 'ricochet' of ambiguities: are we all, cocooned behind glass, the visitors and the visited, on eternal display? Is the here-and-hereafter a transcendable system of endless fluttering and sketching—a chrysalis of ceaselessly transforming beauty and wonder with a snazzy gift shop and café thrown in? Later, on Oxford Street, passing by a bargain shop, I came across a bin of polyester butterflies stapled to cheap elastic bracelets—two for a pound."

JEN HADFIELD lives in Shetland where she works as a writer and tutor. Her first collection *Almanacs* (Bloodaxe, 2005) was written in Shetland and the Western Isles in 2002 thanks to a bursary from the Scottish Arts Council, and it won an Eric Gregory Award in 2003, which enabled her to work on her second collection, *Nigh-No-Place* (Bloodaxe, 2008), in Canada and Shetland. She went on to win the T.S. Eliot Prize for *Nigh-No-Place*, which was also a Poetry Book Society Recommendation as well as being shortlisted for the Forward Prize for Best Collection. She writes, "I've often led a writing workshop drawing on Rabelais' surreal and gargantuan list poem 'The Descriptions of King Lent', but had never tried to write a poem of my own based on it. What I love about it is its scale and hilarity and weirdness; it almost achieves the intimacy of *Gray's Anatomy*. It's like a reversal of the Buddhist meditation on death of the body and the self, too, in which the subject dismantles themselves part by part; in this case body and self get bigger and realler and more insistent with every line. This poem's about my enduring ambition to camouflage myself or dissolve in the natural world, to achieve some kind of invisibility, in this case numbed and then strewn by very cold water. Some day I'll make it much longer, scaling up the dismantlement in particular."

AIKO HARMAN is a Los Angeles native now living in Scotland where she completed an MSc in Creative Writing at the University of Edinburgh. She has also lived in Japan, teaching English to high school students and spending time with her maternal family. Aiko's poetry is published in

Anon, Gutter, and Fuselit, among others. She writes, "*Hitodama* is inspired by a Japanese folkloric icon, the Japanese equivalent of the 'will o' the wisp'. It appears as a ghostly light which is sometimes seen in graveyards or marshland, and which in Japanese culture is often linked to the spirits of the newly dead. I was intrigued to discover that this sort of creature is known by many names in many countries all over the world. In particular I found it interesting how this idea could transcend borders and exist in similar forms across such varied cultures, as if the universality of these primal fears gives rise to shared mythologies. I found myself wondering: do the stories travel or do we somehow arrive at the same results even though we grow up in different worlds? Do we come up with the same stories because ultimately, we're terrified of the same things?"

EMILY HASLER was born in Felixstowe in 1985 and studied for her BA and Masters degrees at Warwick University. In 2009 she was awarded second prize in the Edwin Morgan International Poetry Competition. Her poems appear in *Dove Release: New Flights and Voices* (Worple Press, 2010) and *The Salt Book of Younger Poets* (2011). Her debut pamphlet *Natural Histories* is forthcoming from Salt.

She comments, "I feel guilty that this poem has found its way into a book of poetry from 2010–2011 because this is quite an old poem, or seems so to me. Its origins can be traced back—along a long and embarrassing umbilical of scribblings and semi-poems—to 2004 when I first started at the University of Warwick. I was in a long distance relationship and reading Donne for the first time. I loved his 'Valediction, Forbidding Mourning', especially the idea of the lovers as a parted compass. That image stuck in my head so successfully that I ended up deconstructing it and deciding it was actually a perfect illustration of the gender binary; where the woman remains fixed and acts as a stable other for the man. Why should either partner have to stay in one place? I became annoyed at Donne for having tricked me with a construction so beautifully oiled I didn't notice its machinery. These thoughts became poem and throughout the next year or so I reworked and redrafted this many times.

I am indebted to David Morley who not only encouraged me in my redrafting but first printed the poem, blew it up to A3 size and pinned it on to a notice board on the English department corridor. I discovered with that act, and with this poem, the joy of reaching a point where the poem felt independent of me. That kick is what I've been seeking out in my writing ever since. I'm still working on my feelings toward Donne."

OLI HAZZARD was born in Bristol in 1986. His poetry has appeared or is forthcoming in magazines and anthologies including *The Forward Book of Poetry* 2010, *The Salt Book of Younger Poets* and *New Poetries V* (Carcanet).

He studied English at University College London and Bristol University. He writes of his poem 'Sonnet', "This poem came from having all kinds of half-lines, loose images and truncated narratives that needed somehow to be put away so they would stop trying to wangle their way into my other poems. Restriction appealed: I had to mash in as many things as I could, and what didn't fit would be thrown away. I did a similar thing when moving house last year; now, when I think of all the millions of sonnets that have ever been written, I picture vast warehouses with SELF-STORAGE SOLUTIONS emblazoned on every side in three-hundred foot letters. Being sentimental by nature, I tried to push in more things than there was space for, and probably mangled and broke a few of them in the process. But then most thoughts are improved when warped in their bottling. This is not the case with most furnishings."

W.N. HERBERT was born in 1961 in Dundee. He teaches Creative Writing at Newcastle University and lives in a converted lighthouse in North Shields. He has published a number of collections, the latest being *Bad Shaman Blues* (Bloodaxe, 2006) and he has edited various anthologies and critical works including the poetics anthology *Strong Words: Modern Poets on Modern Poetry*, co-edited with Matthew Hollis. He comments, "'Errant' is an exercise in going wrong—the one thing we can be sure we're entirely competent at. The poem is in seven seven stanza sections, each stanza a slightly 'off' Spenserian—as it developed, I realised even the title was wrong: it's now called 'Pilgrim Street'. Its theme is indeed pilgrimage, or just wandering—something I've done a certain amount of in the last seven years, visiting places from Jerusalem to Djibouti and Kashgar to Caracas, but always travelling as a poet to readings or workshops. This central section looks back at a *nel mezzo del cammin* moment in my thirties when I appeared to be diagnosed with a brain tumour."

ALEXANDER HUTCHISON published *Scales Dog: New and Selected Poems* with Salt in 2007. He has worked mostly in universities, including eighteen years in Canada and the USA, though he gave up being a literary academic some time ago. He lives in Glasgow and currently is RLF Writing Fellow at the Royal Scottish Conservatoire. Last year the distinguished Italian literary journal, *In Forma di Parole* dedicated a complete issue to his work, translated by Alessandro Valenzisi, along with Hutchison's Scots and English versions of Catullus and early Friulian poems by Pier Paolo Pasolini. When he reads in public he likes to work some songs into the mix. He comments, "This poem began its life in English as 'Unfinished Business' and was dedicated to 'CMG'—Christopher Murray Grieve, or Hugh MacDiarmid. A couple of years ago it decided it had another identity, and pretty well transformed itself into (mostly North-east) Scots. The spelling usually is an aid to pronunciation. It should be read out loud, in the spirit of the old flytings: ritual insults freely exchanged. The chopped-out framework and various levels may appear Dantesque, but Dunbar and Rabelais are in the line-up, too."

SARAH JACKSON's debut pamphlet, *Milk* (Pighog, 2008), was shortlisted for the inaugural Michael Marks Poetry Award in 2009, and her work is featured in Bloodaxe's anthology, *Voice Recognition: 21 Poets for the 21st Century* (2009). Sarah has a PhD in Creative and Critical Writing from the University of Sussex and now lectures in English and Creative Writing at Nottingham Trent University, where she is the Programme Leader for the MA in Creative Writing. Her first full-length collection of poetry will be published by Bloodaxe in 2012. She comments, "Walking across the fields near my home in Nottingham, you can see the coal-fired power station at Ratcliffe-On-Soar. The eight cooling towers loom over the landscape with an eerie and unnatural beauty. On some evenings, the gathering of smoke and light produces an almost blinding apocalyptic glare. In this poem, I tried to capture the uncanny strangeness of the light over Rat-cliffe. But this poem isn't just about the strangeness of light; it is also about the strange relationship between writing, blindness and love. People often refer to the ways that love is blind, but I'm also interested in writing as a different way of seeing. Hélène Cixous says: 'I do not want to see what is shown. I want to see what is secret. What is hidden amongst the visible. I want to see the skin of the light.' Writing to see differently, the couplets in this poem follow the ghostly trace of a couple as they walk across the fields at dusk, entering an entirely different field of light."

CHRISTOPHER JAMES was born in Scotland in 1975 and educated at New-castle and UEA, where he graduated with an MA in Creative Writing. He won first prize in the 2008 National Poetry Competition, the Brid-port Prize and the Ledbury Poetry Prize in both 2003 and 2006. He is also the recipient of an Eric Gregory Award. Most recently he was one of three winners of The Templar Poetry Pamphlet & Collection Awards 2011. His first collection *The Invention of Butterfly* (Ragged Raven, 2006) is followed by *Farewell to the Earth* (Arc, 2011) and the pamphlet, *The Manly Art of Knitting* (Templar, 2011). He works as a brand manager and lives in Suffolk with his wife and three young children. He comments, "I heard an item on Radio 4 reporting that eunuchs in New Dehli will now receive a monthly pension—a tiny amount to keep them from begging on the streets. The Hijras, as they are known, sing and dance at wedding ceremonies to bring good luck, but have low social status and suffer an enormous range of problems including violence, illness and poverty. Faced with such stigma and misery I wanted to write a beautiful, joyful poem that describes how their retirement (often beginning as young as 18 years old) could be fulfilled in a way their working life wasn't. I also wanted to celebrate the colour and diversity of India, its rural beauty and modern folk heroes through the travels of a liberated Hijra.

The poem is about redemption; it is a statement of intent—a manifesto to restore dignity after a life of degradation. The Hijra plans to indulge secretly harboured dreams and fantasies—and even at night will wear 'the white headdress shaped like a swan.' The specific detail ('the turquoise stone' and 'striped shirt') aims to show how long this person has dreamt about this moment. Their vision for a blissful retirement is fully formed.

I wanted this sense of freedom and lightness to come through in the sound of the poem; it is filled of airy vowel sounds like 'today', 'crashed', 'dance' and 'grass'; these are offset by the dynamic sibilance of 'kissed' 'silver stilettos' 'city beautiful' which gives the poem energy and vigour—and mirrors the Hijra's determination to transform their life. The framing device (beginning with 'Today' and ending in 'yesterday') also shows how completely the Hijra plans to break from the past.

I realise this is potentially something of a taboo subject, and clearly it bears little resemblance to the reality of the Hijra's difficult lives, but in this dream fantasy I mean to be respectful and celebrate the essential optimism of the human spirit. There is almost a religion dimension to the spiritual journey; in a sense it is a pilgrimage of the self."

Originally from South Africa, KATHARINE KILALEA moved to London in 2005 to study an MA in Creative Writing at the University of East Anglia. Her first book, *One Eye'd Leigh* (Carcanet) was shortlisted for the Costa Poetry Award and longlisted for the Dylan Thomas prize for writers under 30. She has received an Arts Council Award for poetry and her poems have been appeared in publications including the *2010 Forward Prize Anthology*, *PN Review* and *Magma* and performed on the BBC 3, as well as at festivals including the Wordsworth Trust Poetry Festival, Bridlington Poetry Festival and Worlds Literary Festival. A poem on chairs was commissioned for Martino Gamper's design book, *100 Chairs in 100 days and its 100 Ways*. She works as a publicist for an architecture practice in London. She writes, "It is awkward to acknowledge how satisfying I find it to be known by others in a meaningful way and that, for me, the function of writing poems is mostly a selfish pursuit. But the challenge is that the experiences which I wished to write about in this poem—characterised by intense feelings like vulnerability and a sense of indeterminate threat—are irrational and ill-suited to language. Firstly, of course, such experiences are hard to explain, and perhaps more importantly, the desire to write a poem (rather than an essay, say), reveals a desire to do more than just describe them. Beyond a certain threshold of intensity, explaining is not enough—so, when I am very angry, I don't want to be *understood*, I want to fight, or if I feel love, I want to seduce, etc. I think this desire to infect others with an experience is the logic of 'Hennecker's Ditch'. On the surface, it seems a difficult poem, but it's only hard work when you try to make it meaningful."

NICK LAIRD is a poet, novelist and critic, and was born in County Tyrone in 1975. His debut collection *To A Fault* (Faber, 2005) won the Rooney Prize for Irish literature, the Jerwood Aldeburgh Prize and the Ireland Chair of Poetry Prize. *On Purpose* (Faber, 2007) was awarded a Somerset Maugham Award and the Geoffrey Faber Memorial Prize. A new collection *Go Giants* will be published next year. He teaches at Barnard College in New York and writes an occasional column on poetry for the *Guardian*. He writes, "I'm not too happy at paraphrasing or explaining things but the poem's about growing up in Co. Tyrone, and what was in my mind in the first stanza was the Teebane bombing, in which a friend of mine died and which happened at a 'treeless crossroads' near my house. The poem asks a few heavily disguised questions about responsibility and connivance, and I suppose there's a sharp elbow aimed at Yeats there, with the line about all ceremony being a hoax. In 'Prayer for My Daughter' he wrote 'How but in custom and in ceremony are innocence and beauty born?' Well, actually custom and ceremony are the very things complicit in maintaining the status quo in the North of Ireland. The habituation of violence. The head-down acceptance and collusion of the churches and the state, the segregated schooling systems etc. Northern Ireland is pretty singular; its democracy entirely subsumed by identity-based politics founded on rival interpretations of the bible, and to that end the last stanza tries to use the Beaghmore stone circles near where I grew up, (and which blackface and cheviot sheep wander round, getting on with their ovine business) as an analogy for way the lives of ordinary people are overlaid or circumscribed by ancient structures. But when I write it out like that it all sounds a bit schematic."

PIPPA LITTLE was born in East Africa, raised in Scotland and now lives in Northumberland. She has a PhD in contemporary women's poetry and has worked as an editor, literacy tutor and lecturer. *The Spar Box* (Vane Women, 2006) was a PBS Pamphlet Choice. *Foray, Border Reiver Women* was published by Biscuit Press in 2009 and *The Snow Globe* will be published by Red Squirrel Press in 2011. *Overwintering* will be published 2012 by Oxford Poets/Carcanet. She notes, "I wrote this while staying on a sheep farm in Northumberland. It had been a tough winter. Weakling lambs were lain under a heat lamp in the barn. The motherless were wrapped in the fleece shorn from a dead lamb and given to the lost one's mother in the hope that she would suckle it, thinking it was her own. Being there reminded me of my childhood in Fife, and I wrote this very quickly. I'm not sure where it came from, and why it came out as a sonnet. It feels a bit mysterious, There are Scots words and Northumbrian mixed together: these are both my languages now. Billy Blin is a Borders/ Northumbrian 'home spirit' believed to guard against hard luck. It's a special poem for me as it won the Norman MacCaig Centenary Poetry Prize and gave me the wonderful experience of sharing the celebrations up in Assynt on a writing retreat I shall never forget."

CHRIS MCCABE was born in Liverpool in 1977. His first collection *The Hutton Inquiry* was published by Salt in 2005, which *The Guardian* reviewed as "an impressively inventive survey of the uses of English in the early 21st century". This was followed by *Zeppelins* in 2008 and a pamphlet of ludic elegies in memory of his dad—called *The Borrowed Notebook*—in 2009. He has also recorded a CD with The Poetry Archive. In 2010 he wrote *Shad Thames, Broken Wharf*, a play about the London Docklands which was performed at the London Word Festival and at the Bluecoat in Liverpool. This is available as a limited edition book from Penned in the Margins. His next book *THE RESTRUCTURE* will be published by Salt in 2012. He comments as follows, "For years I've dreamt about the kingfisher, a shriek of electric blue in the skewed eidetic underworld. As well as being the bird I couldn't see, the kingfisher was also the poem I couldn't write. The kingfisher represents the synaesthesia-in-flight that is in the kind of nature poetry I go for (Hopkins, Hughes, Langley). I thought I needed to see the bird first—to manifest the dream—before the poem could happen. When he was born our son brought his parents the pleasure of birdwatching. He closed the nestbox on pubs: he couldn't have been older than a few months when he was cradled next to us as we finished a Wetherspoons' lunch. His face creased into a fiery red boozer's grimace. He didn't like it there.

We switched stimuli to the habitat of the birds. Rainham Marshes. Eastbrookend Country Park. It was more surreal than any vino session to watch my wife, an urban girl (who'd walked the Port of Liverpool's cobbles in Doc Martens) stumble curiously into rhododendrons. On our family twitches, which were her moments off from parental duties, I would leave her to lose herself in nature as I grabbed the reins on the growing boy. And that's when my dream was her nerve-rush. Not one—but two—kingfishers, darting from a bush to the banks of the lake. I was dealing with the boy's missing shoe, or marshy nappy, and missed the moment. It was the boy that brought me the near-experience of the kingfisher (even on the beer front I'll take a Cobra before a Kingfisher).

But this was no near-miss: the bird and I had passed each other for a reason. That night, the poem started to twitch in a mossy nest of bone-brittle syntax. Only not seeing the bird could make the poem happen. And my son — that trickster of ruse diversions — seemed to know that — from the smirk of irony in his quick blue eyes."

TED MCCARTHY lives and teaches in Clones, Ireland. His work has appeared in various magazines and anthologies in Ireland, Britain, Europe, Australia and the U.S. He has had one collection, 'November Wedding' published; a second is due out later this year. He has also written a number of scripts for short films and one-act plays, and has been on judging panels for several film and literary festivals. Shooting on a film *The Suitcase* is due to begin in early 2012. He comments, "A couple of years ago, I spent a brief spell as writer-in-residence at an establishment in Dublin. It was, in a way, a period of self-imposed exile, during which I watched the mundane comings and goings in adjoining housing estates. The view from the inside looking out. The poem was written about a year later. This time I was looking in: and not just at where I'd been geographically. Many perspectives had altered for me in the intervening time. My recollection of that stay in Dublin was beginning to, if not fade, then distort slightly. I needed to root myself again in the ideas, the sensations, the possibilities I'd experienced.

Sometimes the act of remembering resembles nothing as much as a game of Chinese whispers — remembering a memory of a memory, and so on, back to the pinpoint of what really happened, the actuality of what it was like at the time. This poem, and others like it, give me a sense of immediacy, so that when I read it I'm back there. A fleeting but necessary visit."

JOHN MCCULLOUGH's poetry has appeared in publications including *London Magazine, The Guardian, The Rialto, Poetry London* and *Magma*. He teaches creative writing for the Open University, the University of Sussex, the Poetry School and the Arvon Foundation. He lives in Hove. He writes, "'Sleeping Hermaphrodite' became the opening poem of my first collection *The Frost Fairs* (Salt, 2011). I really wanted to begin the book with a piece that takes an unexpected angle as that's something central to my kind of writing; I enjoy exploring perspectives that are surreal yet at the same time still carry an emotional resonance. In many ways, the poem is itself about the nature of being caught off guard. The speaker seems asleep but isn't, appears to be female but isn't — and yet s/he isn't male either. How does it feel to defy categories at such a fundamental level? In the last six lines, the narrator also switches and suddenly becomes much more intimate, ardent and, indeed, downright cheeky.

The sonnet is an ideal form for a piece about confounding expectations because of the 'turn' between lines 8 and 9 that frequently involves some kind of deepening or contradiction of what's been said so far. I chose to write it in slant rhyme because this, too, involves the reader encountering unusual pairings that chime in an offbeat way, both rhyming and not rhyming. *The Frost Fairs* is a collection interested in hidden histories, including the stories of gay, transgender and intersex lives, so this poem prepares the reader for what's to come later. Seeing the famous 'Sleeping Hermaphrodite' statue in The Louvre—which very much seems like a traditional female until you take a closer look—made me want to write in the voice of this particular intersex individual. I wanted the poem to retain a sense of mystery at the end so deliberately left some unanswered questions. Are we listening to a statue or a real person? And how might the 'you' of the piece respond to this address? I'll leave you to decide . . ."

PATRICK MCGUINNESS was born in Tunisia in 1968 and is now Professor of French and Comparative Literature at the University of Oxford, where he is a Fellow of St Anne's College. He is the author of two collections of poems, The Canals of Mars and Jilted City (both published by Carcanet), a novel, *The Last Hundred Days*, and several academic books about French literature and modern poetry. In 2009 he was made Chevalier des Palmes académiques for services to French culture, and in 2011 Chevalier des Arts et des Lettres. He lives in Caernarfon, Wales. He comments, "This poem has a pretty obvious premise, and one we all—most of us—can relate to. It appears in my second full collection, *Jilted City*, a book whose pattern only emerged after I saw it all printed up on the page: it's a book of endings. All kinds of endings: the end of a trainline (the 'Ligne 162' that links my family home in Belgium with Brussels), my lost Belgian childhood, the ends of relationships and the deaths of my nearest if not always (some of them at any rate) dearest.

'House Clearance' is about the emptying of the family home. I say my childhood is lost, yes, and that's obvious. But the childhood home isn't, I still live there, and keep catching the ghost of myself as a child. First my grandparents died, and I cleared the house with my parents, and then my parents died and I cleared it with my partner, and with our own children. It's hard not to feel that we're in some recurrent pattern. Also, when one clears a house, one is also deciding what to keep. So the place feels empty and full at the same time, because what you keep is what means most to you. So you end up thinking you're clearing a space, but in fact you're filling yourself up more intensely with what, perhaps, you ought to be leaving behind.

The last few lines allude to the way in which, heartbreakingly, you always find pictures of yourself on the walls and shelves of the people who have died. So there too you're seeing the ghost of yourself. In the end it's just you, the 'last flame in the grate', in your theatre of shadows (i.e. ghosts), and you're Hamlet because they're all in your head now. That's the only place they exist."

KONA MACPHEE grew up in Australia, where she experimented with a range of occupations including composer, violinist, waitress and motor-cycle mechanic. Eventually she took up robotics and computer science, which brought her to Cambridge as a graduate student in 1995. She now lives in Scotland, where she works as a freelance writer and moonlights as the co-director of a software and consultancy company. She has two col-lections published by Bloodaxe Books, *Tails* (2004) and *Perfect Blue* (2010) which won the 2010 Geoffrey Faber Memorial Prize, and she received an Eric Gregory award in 1998. She writes, "In 1988, I saw a movie called *Crossing Delancey*. I can't remember a thing about it apart from the fact that it was a formulaic and (evidently) forgettable RomCom. Somehow, in my own head, *Crossing Delancey* now epitomises the whole B Movie phenom-enon: films, of whatever genre, that are considered marketable enough for a cinema release precisely because their tropes are so well-worn, their plot devices so reassuringly familiar, their narrative arcs so diligently pre-trodden by a thousand similar B Movies before them.

In 'My life as a B Movie', I enjoyed subverting some of those RomCom clichés and finishing on a darker note than the Hollywood Happy Ending ever allows. As I wrote it, I kept thinking of actress Joan Cusack (sister of John), who's so often been cast (and woefully under-used) in those best friend / sister / secretary supporting roles. The poem's almost cer-tainly inspired by Roddy Lumsden's '364', whose closing lines have been dancing around in my head for years:

> Later, when they make a film of this,
> my character is younger, handsome
> and altogether missing from that scene.

It's also a bit of a hat-tip to screenwriter Charlie Kaufman, author of such convention-mangling and brain-tingling screenplays as *Being John Malko-vich* and in particular 'Adaptation', which presents its own frenetic riffs on some B Movie clichés."

LORRAINE MARINER was born in 1974 and lives in London where she works at the Poetry Library, Southbank Centre. In 2007 her poem 'Thurs-day' was shortlisted for the Forward Prize for Best Single Poem. Her col-lection *Furniture* was published by Picador in 2009 and shortlisted for the Forward Prize for Best First Collection and the Seamus Heaney Centre

Poetry Prize. She writes, "About eight years ago I ate a meal outside in a garden on a summer's evening and when the meal was over I looked back at the table where we had been sitting from the other end of the garden. Seeing the table from that removed perspective I had something of a 'Wow' moment, thinking, 'Wow, I was just sitting at that table in the evening sun, in this beautiful garden, eating fantastic food with my fantastic friend . . .' The image stayed with me and a couple of years ago someone close to me was trying to keep their relationship going after their partner had had an affair and I wrote this poem. I love the mystery of Paul Muldoon's poem 'Why Brownlee Left' and I was trying to write a poem where it was up to the reader who the people in the poem were and what had been going on. The poem also allowed me to use the word "nonsense". At the time I had been thinking about that phrase where you describe someone as being a 'no-nonsense' person but that we don't exactly have an opposite phrase for people at the other end of the nonsense spectrum."

SOPHIE MAYER is a writer, teacher and bookseller, currently based in London. She is the author of *Her Various Scalpels* (Shearsman, 2009) and *The Private Parts of Girls* (Salt, 2011), as well as the critical book *The Cinema of Sally Potter: A Politics of Love* (Wallflower, 2009). She is a member of the editorial teams of *Chroma* and *Hand+Star*, and a regular contributor to *Sight & Sound*. Current projects include further research into the legacy of the St. Ives artists, and particularly the potter Bernard Leach. She writes, "The poem started out as an ekphrastic response to two paintings on display at Tate St. Ives: an abstract painting by Roger Hilton and a seascape through a window by Winifred Nicholson. Formally, it's the meeting of the influence of two Modernist poets on my writing: Lorine Niedecker and Gertrude Stein, whose work was particularly shaped by her encounters with modern art.

But looking at the paintings in the place where they were painted began to merge the landscapes represented and the landscapes I was walking through and looking at: I was transfixed by the gallery's porthole window overlooking the shoreline on a blustery winter day. The meshing of the gallery, the sea and the paintings—the sense of being in, or moving between, them by looking—blurred outside and inside, creating a sense of suspension. The poem takes its title from 'Des autres espaces,' a beautiful lecture Michel Foucault gave shortly before he died. In it, he described what he called heterotopia, other spaces, but also spaces of otherness. He talks about how gardens, ships, and galleries (among other spaces) create a sense of being outside the world; how they layer onto each other, so that any gallery evokes time spent in other galleries; and how they include seemingly impossible spaces within them, as if each painting were an entrance onto a distant landscape. So the poem wants to blur the frame, melt the wall, and bring together the painting, the gallery and the world."

GORDON MEADE lives in the East Neuk of Fife where he divides his time between his own writing and running creative writing courses for vulnerable young people. At present, he is one of the Royal Literary Fund Writing Fellows at the University of Dundee. His sixth collection *The Familiar* was published in Spring 2011 by Arrowhead Press. He writes, "A large number of my poems take, as their starting points, descriptions of animals or birds and then play with the similarities between the animal and human worlds. Other poems, primarily place-based, take off from descriptions of particular locations and move on towards more general observations about the influences certain environments may have on people.

Rats takes aspects of both these approaches. In this poem, the non-specific *here*, although definitely Western European, remains intentionally ambiguous. *Here*, the civilised ideals of efficiency and cleanliness are poked fun at, initially, by citing them as grounds for the dissolution of human relationships. They are further highlighted by examining the underbelly of human society in the form of the rats. Again, as in my other animal poems, I intended to remain ambiguous in my presentation of the rats, leaving it up to the reader to decide how human or non-human the rats in this particular poem might be."

MATT MERRITT is a poet and wildlife journalist from near Leicester. His most recent collection is *hydrodaktulopsychicharmonica* (Nine Arches, 2010), while previous publications were *Troy Town* (2008) and *Making The Most Of The Light* (2005). He is a co-editor of the website Poets On Fire and has reviewed poetry for *Magma*, *New Welsh Review* and *Under The Radar*. He writes, "The title, the first part of the scientific name of the Golden Plover, was very much the starting point for this poem. It means 'bringing rain', reflecting the fact that the birds arrive in lowland Britain in large numbers just ahead of autumn storms, and so were once considered to foretell the weather.

Here, I wanted to turn that around a little and instead associate them with change, of all sorts. On the concrete level, that's there in their fresh spring plumage, and that entirely predictable annual transformation contrasts with their seemingly sudden decision to depart as a flock, fleeing the rain.

Suspense was the other main driving force. Something is about to happen throughout the poem, to the nervous birds, the irritable fisherman, the lovers wrapped up in each other, and the observer/narrator, and as much as anything the poem's about the pleasure of sudden release, contrasting with the tension that waiting for harbingers (such as weather-predicting birds) builds.

Finally, I was entirely unconscious of the fact the first and last words rhyme until I'd revised the poem twice. I'd love to claim it was wholly intentional, but in fact it was one of those happy accidents that happen in poetry."

KATE MILLER lives and works in London, a graduate of Cambridge and London Universities. Her first poems were written at evening classes at Morley College and in 2008, her poem 'After the Ban' won the Edwin Morgan Prize. From 2007 to 2011 she studied for a PhD at Goldsmiths, while slowly assembling a first collection. She comments, "From the Greek port of Volos, the road east climbs Mount Pilion (once, they say, home to centaurs) and wriggles down to the coast through orchards satisfying a big export trade in fruit juice, partly because the rock bursts with natural springs and partly because of the liberal use of fertiliser. Enormous fruits and local vegetables are piled high at roadside stalls and village shops. Look inside the shop and in the shadow of a shelf you expect to see a picture or statuette of the Holy Virgin but a naked Eve is another matter, especially one so reverently kept.

I am interested in observances, the tiny rituals of everyday, by which we honour household gods or sacred images. Here something is happening between a man and a painted woman, grubby and reproduced. This fruit seller continually invests (what?—I don't know, admiration?) in his beautiful nude and derives pleasure from her. I tried to preserve the detail of their little ballet of mutual acknowledgment, in the way he takes his cue from her and handles his produce with infinite care, the simplest of packaging, a way of doing things that must be ages old."

ESTHER MORGAN's first book, *Beyond Calling Distance* (Bloodaxe, 2001), won the Aldeburgh Poetry Festival First Collection prize and was short-listed for the John Llewellyn Rhys Memorial Prize. Her third collection, Grace, will be published in autumn 2011. She lives in Norfolk where she works in the museum world and as an editor for the Poetry Archive. She comments, "As a veteran of rented accommodation I was interested in exploring that tenuous sense of occupation when you first move into a new property which isn't your own. The trigger for this particular poem came when my husband and I moved back to Norfolk after several years away. It occurred to me on that first night that anyone peering through a window into the house at all the unpacked boxes could equally assume we'd just moved in or were about to move out. I liked that sense of ambiguity and provisionality—none of our possessions had yet found their 'place', everything felt adrift, unmoored. What were our lives going to be like in this new environment? There's a sense of threat in this lack of rootedness but also of opportunity too—that's what I hope is conveyed by the final image. I suppose beyond the immediate context of the poem is a broader feeling that our lives are always transitional, incomplete, that our time here is only ever a tenancy and not a permanent home."

CATHERINE ORMELL is a director of a small design consultancy. She trained as a journalist and wrote features for *The Daily Telegraph, The Independent, The Times Educational Supplement* and *World Architecture* amongst others. Her poems have been published in many magazines including, *The Spectator, The London Magazine, The Rialto* and *Smiths Knoll*. Her poem Campaign Desk was shortlisted for the Forward prize for best poem and is in the 2009 anthology. She writes, "The château in question really exists; it's in Aquitaine, deep in French plum country. By day, it's idyllic, if isolated, but at night an unhappy atmosphere builds up in the house. We rented it for a holiday but after a week we were so unnerved (and unslept) we moved into a local hotel. Later we discovered that the house had been owned by the same family from the eleventh century through to the First World War when all of the four sons were killed (I slipped 1914 into the timing of the birdscarer). For most of the twentieth century the château was uninhabited but at the time of our visit, it was being done-up by a couple from Paris. Generally I try to avoid ghosts in poems but in this case my unconscious caught me out; the haunting transferred to the plums.

I'm particularly fond of Dr Johnson's observation '*Nothing is more hopeless than a scheme of merriment,*' and we had to take the holiday in that spirit which probably accounts for the poem's tone. The act of writing was a Saturday evening bath-to-laptop special; after ten years of gestation, it pretty much threw itself onto the page and in revising it I only needed to tweak the order of the fawn and the moon and tighten-up the closing image."

RICHARD OSMOND was born in 1987. He studied English at Queens' College, Cambridge and will soon be studying for a Masters Degree in Creative Writing at the University of St Andrews. He was a Foyle Young Poet of the Year in 2005 and his poetry was included in the anthology *the mays xviii* (Varsity Publications, 2010). He writes the following, "This poem was originally meant to serve as an overture to a longer work. On holiday to the Suffolk coast, I thought of writing a poem sequence recounting the history of Suffolk from its prosperous medieval period through to the present day. Additionally, I drunkenly planned each poem's style and themes would be modelled after a different beer produced by Adnams—the brewery whose pubs hold something of a monopoly in the area.

Jack o' the clock is a funny little wooden figure in medieval armour who rings the clock bell at St Edmund's church in Southwold. He has also been adopted by Adnams as brand logo and symbol of the company's place in traditional, idyllic Suffolk. With 'Logo', Jack also becomes the figure-head of my poetic project and the speaker of its introduction, presiding with historical omniscience over a series of blurry snapshots of East Anglia. Coastal erosion, the wool-trade, Sizewell B and the reformation all surface briefly before fading away beneath the chimes of the church clock. The rest of the sequence, of course, was never finished. I never researched or expanded upon the themes in 'Logo', so this slight, impressionistic flurry of images is all that remains. Far from serving as heroic blazon for a grand pub crawl through history, my Jack is alone, and rings his bell forlornly out to sea, an orphaned signifier like Greyfriars Monastery, which stands on the receding cliffs at Dunwich, its diocese and congregation long since lost to the waves."

RUTH PADEL has published seven poetry collections, most recently *Darwin—A Life in Poems*, shortlisted for the Costa Award. Her books on reading poems include *Silent Letters of the Alphabet* on poetry's use of silence; her novel *Where the Serpent Lives* was praised in Britain and India especially for its nature writing. Her awards include First Prize in the National Poetry Competition and she is Fellow of both the Royal Society of Literature and Zoological Society of London. *The Mara Crossing*, forthcoming 2012, and containing 'Only Here on Earth' puts today's migrations in the wider context of cells, trees, birds, and human history.

She writes, "The lines quoted at the beginning come from the Aztec poet Nezahualcoyotl. I came across them in a newspaper article and was touched by how fresh and direct they were, what a *cri du coeur* about being remembered—or not—over the centuries. They seemed to me to sum up one thing poets always long for—to be: heard by other people. He lived before the Spanish Conquest, 1403–1472. As a fifteen year old prince he fled to exile when the Tepanecs, a rival tribe from the kingdom of Azcapotzalco, conquered his kingdom of Texcoco. He returned to Texcoco but had to go into exile again, with plots against his life in what sounded to me, as I looked up this colour-filled history, like an Aztec Wars of the Roses. He formed a coalition with other pre-Hispanic cities and led an army of 100,000 to reconquer his city. Later, revered as the philosopher-king, a poet, architect and sage (but always, I noticed, a warrior too) he created Texcoco's Golden Age, bringing law, scholar-ship and art to 'the Athens of the Western World,' with hilltop gardens, sculpture and a massive aqueduct system.

Well, that's what the books say, but what drew me in were his words. For six years now, I've been thinking and writing poems about migration in all its forms, biological and historical, birds, trees and people. In writing this poem, something about writers in exile, about his words in connection with his life, mapped themselves onto a sunlit moment of my own in a kitchen and a garden."

EMMA PAGE was born in 1973. She lives in south east London where she divides her time between looking after her son and working as an education writer and literacy consultant. She has been a reader and writer of poetry all her life and enjoys attending readings, courses and workshops whenever she can. 'California' was her first published poem. She comments as follows, "My hire-car travels around California with my husband are among my most cherished holiday memories and I returned from our more recent holiday there with several pages of notebook jottings but little sense of direction about what to do with them. A couple of years later, I had an idea that the stack of gold purses I'd seen in San Francisco's Chinatown and written about in my notes could be the starting point for a travel poem of sorts, a poem that's concerned with the provenance and onward journey of the thing it describes. Indeed the drafting of the poem went on its own unexpected journey, veering away from my notes and instead taking inspiration from a documentary, a news story, a movie. The resulting poem is an effort to weave together some stories from a long commodity chain and manufacture my own small souvenir."

NII AYIKWEI PARKES is a Ghanaian writer and a 2007 recipient of Ghana's national ACRAG award for poetry. His poetry pamphlet, *ballast: a remix*, was shortlisted for the 2009 Michael Marks Award and his novel *Tail of the Blue Bird* (Jonathan Cape, 2009), was shortlisted for the 2010 Commonwealth Prize. Nii has held visiting positions at the University of Southampton and California State University and serves on the board of the Poetry Book Society. His latest book of poems is *The Makings of You* (Peepal Tree, 2010). He comments, "There's nothing like the inside of a coach on a darkening day for drawing the eye to light and small details. The little spotlights above each seat can make it seem like everyone is on stage; that's precisely how it seemed to me when I woke up on a New York-bound coach after a reading in Connecticut. Awareness came to me in little bursts and the drama outlined in the poem played out before me. Thinking about it later, it struck me how the little possibility of romance I had witnessed mirrored the nature of opportunity in life itself, so I made up the conversation of the man beside me, who was actually arranging to meet some friends in Times Square that night. I chose to use three-line stanzas to reflect the measured manner in which realisation hit me, and I tried to end the lines to both emphasise words and add nuance."

ABIGAIL PARRY lives in London, and is currently working towards a PhD in poetics. She has published poems in various journals and anthologies, and received an Eric Gregory Award in 2010. She is a toymaker by profession. She comments, "As wary as I am of poems 'about writing poems', I should confess that 'Hare' is precisely that. It grew out of my revisions for another poem, one cluttered with clumsy polysyllables that were, nonetheless, semantically economical: they nailed the point I'd been trying to make. It was this that sounded the warning bell. A poem, I realised, should never 'get to the point'.

This skirting around an idea, never losing sight of it but also never pouncing on it directly, reminded me of something I was once told about catching a hare. See him in a field, make straight for him, and he'll bolt. You must, apparently, walk in ever-decreasing rings around him. By the time you're on top of him, he won't have known which way to run, and you'll have him. This seemed to me a perfect metaphor for the poetic process, and I wrote 'Hare' as a result. I wished to create something that reflected this process of discovery—where free verse gives way to established meter as the pattern appears, and the rhythm quickens as one gets closer to success (or the realisation, or the end). It's the process describing itself.

A unicursal, circuitous path towards a central point is a labyrinth by any other name, and the ground to be mined there is rich indeed. Labyrinths were used in antiquity to achieve contemplative states, or fertility. They were paths for ritual dances, especially for virgins (this furnished me with my closing couplet); they have also been used to trap spirits. The Hare as Muse, meanwhile, is by no means unusual. In animal lore he is the Trickster, an archetype associated with creation and rebirth; he's the totem of the coming spring, of fecundity. In many depictions he appears positively lecherous—and let's be honest, he's a sexy beast. A wary, quasi-sexual relationship, where destruction is essential to creation—this seems to me accurately to describe the relationship of poet to poem. I say destruction, because something is conquered, or resolved, in the creative process—something is dispelled."

ANDREW PHILIP was born in Aberdeen in 1975 and grew up near Falkirk. He lives near Edinburgh and works for the Scottish Parliament. His first full collection *The Ambulance Box* was published by Salt in 2009. It was shortlisted for the Aldeburgh First Collection Prize 2009, the Scottish Arts Council First Book Award 2010 and the inaugural Seamus Heaney Centre Prize for Poetry. He writes, "This sequence, written as a present for my wife, is organised by direct or oblique reference to a list of anniversary gifts for the first 10 years of marriage: paper, cotton, leather, linen, wood, iron, copper, bronze, linen, pottery and tin. Each poem moves through each of the 10 gifts in turn line by line. Each successive poem begins with the gift for the corresponding anniversary (so number 1 starts with paper, number 2 with cotton and so forth). Every poem's title alludes to the relevant gift, which is also the one word banned from appearing directly in the poem. In a gesture drawn from the sonnet, there is generally a turn—a shift in the poem's tone or argument—in, or just before, the second stanza of each piece."

HEATHER PHILLIPSON works across moving image, poetry, sound and live events. As an artist, she exhibits nationally and internationally and has received awards, commissions and residencies. In 2011, she has shown work at the ICA (London), Hollybush Gardens (London), Halle 14 (Leipzig), KG52 Gallery (Stockholm), Eastside Projects (Birmingham) and the South London Gallery. In parallel, her poems have been published widely in magazines and anthologies. She received an Eric Gregory Award in 2008, a Faber New Poets award in 2009 and an ACE bursary in 2011. Her pamphlet is published by Faber and Faber. She writes, "It is hard to say anything that is as good as saying nothing. Babies confirm this. When my niece was born, I realized I knew nothing about babies, or anything else really. Poetry, for me, is mainly not-knowing. In a state of incompleteness, something remains possible. So, when my niece was born, I wrote a poem. Little happens. Little that I could explain anyway.

I could tell you that the poem is made in the way department stores sell off their winter jumpers. I could tell you that I liquidated my current stock of unverifiable postulations and what you see is the car boot sale. This is its point. Nearly all ideas come ready-crumpled. I didn't know where the poem was going. Things rubbed together. It was risky. It necessitated making and avoiding choices. It proceeded from half-digested notions propped up with contradictory information. Let's call it an attempt—to speculate, to converse, to disrobe. It involved a couple of images that provoked me, words too. Apparently, you ought to be able to start with nothing but your own minor reality and end with an approximation of art.

What I would say is that, like Claes Oldenburg, I am for an art that unfolds like a map, that you can squeeze, like your sweetie's arm, or kiss, like a pet dog. Which expands and squeaks, like an accordion, which you can spill your dinner on, like an old tablecloth. I am for an art that embroils itself with the everyday crap and still comes out on top. I would say that I'd never imagined I'd write a poem with a baby in it. But then a baby came along and I thought: why not? Babies exist."

KATE POTTS lives in London. Her debut pamphlet *Whichever Music* (tall-lighthouse) was a Poetry Book Society Choice in 2008 and was shortlisted for a Michael Marks Award. Her work was featured in the Bloodaxe anthology *Voice Recognition* in 2009 and her first full length collection *Pure Hustle* was published by Bloodaxe in 2011. She is currently studying for a PhD on radio poetry plays. She comments, "The starting point for 'Three Wishes' was a news story about a teenage girl who claimed to have fallen asleep at the tattoo parlour and woken to find 56 stars engraved on her face rather than the three she'd requested. The story reminded me of a short story, 'Planetesimal,' by the New Zealand author Keri Hulme, in which a particular tattoo-like mark on the skin is part of a very strange and sinister sort of sickness.

I'd been reading and rereading Angela Carter's Virago collections of fairy tales, as well as translations of the tales written down by Charles Perrault, Giambattista Basile and the Brothers Grimm, and thinking about how the wishes and desires that drive their characters relate to my world today: how far have our obsessions—and the way they manifest themselves—shifted? I wrote the first section of the poem as an extended list of wishes, mixing fairy tale images with contemporary ones. In the end, the poem became a sort of cautionary tale about the idea of progress and the complex and unpredictable reality involved in getting what we wish for."

VIDYAN RAVINTHIRAN is a lecturer at Oxford and a research fellow at Cambridge. Among other magazines, his poems have appeared or are forthcoming in *Poetry Review, The Times Literary Supplement, The Rialto, Magma, The North, Blackbox Manifold, Ambit, Poetry Wales, Stand, Nthposition, Likestarlings, Poetry Proper, Fuselit, Oxford Poetry, Iota, Horizon Review and Smiths Knoll*; they have been anthologised in *Joining Music With Reason* (Waywiser Press, 2010) and *The Salt Book of Younger Poets* (Salt, 2011). A pamphlet of his work, *At Home or Nowhere*, was published by tall-lighthouse Press in 2008. He comments, "We often talk about the experience of reading in physical, rather than intellectual terms. There are perhaps two reasons for this. On the one hand, we want to insist on the elements of that experience which cannot be reconciled with an ideal of disinterested aesthetic contemplation. Reading always stirs up entirely personal associations on the part of the reader, and literary texts provoke lust, shock and horror just as powerfully (or more so) than any Mills and Boon or penny dreadful.

That we refer to literature (novels, especially) as 'gripping' or 'heartstopping' or 'spine-tingling' has also, however, to do with the need to market such works, brutally. In this sense, such terminology is reductive—it tries to sell books to us by reassuring us that, like summer blockbusters, literature doesn't demand any mental activity whatsoever for its proper reception. Instead, it's like a ride on a rollercoaster, doing crazy things to our bodies. My poem represents an attempt to think through this problem."

DERYN REES-JONES has published three collections of poetry with Seren, most recently *Quiver*. *Burying the Wren* is forthcoming in 2012. She is the author of a critical book on twentieth-century women's poetry, *Consorting with Angels* and the editor of the accompanying anthology, *Modern Women Poets*. She teaches literature at the University of Liverpool. She writes, "Who is Elisabeth So? I'm not sure. At one point while writing these poems she had assumed a whole biography, and was about to publish her first book of poems. Now it seems she's left, her belongings scattered across my desk, a biro on the windowsill, a half-empty glass of wine balanced precariously on a radiator. Infuriating as a houseguest, she'd leave taps running, windows open when the house was empty; she'd boil kettles and then forget to make the tea . . . She clearly loved my children deeply, but always kept them at a strategic remove. The poems here are moments from a past she's broken with; written in haste, translated from her first language. I was glad to find them: a slightly tattered sheaf of papers tucked rather more neatly than I'd have supposed on a bookshelf in my study. Unassuming in the end, and waiting to be found."

SAM RIVIERE co-edits the anthology series *Stop Sharpening Your Knives*, and was a recipient of a 2009 Eric Gregory Award. Faber & Faber published his pamphlet in 2010 as part of their New Poets scheme. *81 Austerities*, a collection of poems responding to the arts cuts is available online. He comments, "I hate it when people say this, but this poem was based on a dream I had. I have never been to Las Vegas, but the dream seemed set in some version of Vegas. In the dream I didn't seem to know my bride either, a fact she drew my attention to at some point. The poem works like the dream, various details are revealed as the story progresses, which might dramatically alter the situation somehow. This can happen in a poem — you can suddenly reveal your conversation is taking place on the back of an elephant — in the same way that a situation can abruptly change in a dream. It's probably true that saying in the poem that 'it was all a dream' is a bad idea though. Perhaps dreams are so weird because they have to go to such drastic lengths to create a situation that produces their specific feeling. Freud said all dreams are wish fulfilment, and it sounds believable that reproducing while simultaneously disguising a feeling is the driving force of a dream's narrative. So bad things might happen in dreams (the vanished parents maybe) so that a desired scenario or feeling can come into being.

In the poem the bride announces what everything 'means' as it happens, sort of like an indicator of potential plot developments, as if the dream is self-conscious about its own machinations. Once we get to the scene that might appear to be the 'goal' of the story however, meaning or desire peters out, and I guess we are left to go back to try and locate the point of the encounter, the moment that the fantasy permits, among the accumulation of details. The remark about the lilies was made to me by someone after I had stolen some flowers from a 'Welcome Break' service station, and I'd wanted to use it in a poem for ages."

COLETTE SENSIER is from Brighton and has been writing since she was a teenager. She has been a winner of the Foyle's, Tower and Peterloo young poets' prizes, and has been published in magazines including *The Rialto, South, Iota, Frogmore Papers* and *Horizon*. Her work was featured in anthologies *Asking A Shadow to Dance: 30 Young Poets for Oxfam* and *Poetry South-East 2010*, and she has poems in *The Salt Book of Younger Poets*. Of Orpheus, she comments, "This poem was inspired by a Tower Poetry workshop a few years ago, where we worked on relocating a myth to a different landscape. I used the myth of Orpheus, who visits the Underworld to find the love of his life, the dead Eurydice. His lyre playing charmed the inhabitants of Hell and he was allowed to take Eurydice back to the land of the living, but on the condition that he doesn't look back at her as they travel. He fails and looks back at her, and she disappears back into Hell. However, the 'pomegranate seeds' in the third part of the poem refer to another woman almost saved from the Underworld, Persephone, who can only live in the real world for half of the year, in the summertime, as she ate six pomegranate seeds while living in Hell.

I have family in Mauritius, and had visited once before, but the poet John Clegg's description of his recent visit to Mahebourg Market inspired a lot of the poem. The poem is about the possibility of finding answers—nothing as concrete as Eurydice really exists to be found when you're thinking about a place or a strand of your heritage. The market reflects the multiculturality of Mauritius, which has inhabitants of African, South Asian, European, Chinese and mixed heritage. Although all three parts are in free verse, they are quite different in form. The first part is in third person, second in first person, and third in second person, and they're different visually, as the first part has long thin lines, the second is brief, and the third in the middle."

PENELOPE SHUTTLE was born in Staines and has lived in Cornwall since 1970. She has published eight collections, including a *Selected Poems* in 1998. *Redgrove's Wife* was shortlisted for the Forward and the TS Eliot prizes. Her ninth collection, *Sandgrain and Hourglass* (Bloodaxe, 2010) was a PBS Recommendation. It was a Poetry Book of the Year in *The Financial Times*. With her late husband Peter Redgrove, she is co-author of *The Wise Wound* (1978). Her *New and Selected Poems* are in preparation and will appear from Bloodaxe in 2013.

She writes, "This poem is part of a series of loosely connected poems

I'm writing on the theme of 'the year', and includes 'The Seventh Year' (*Poetry Review*) and 'Quiet Year' (*Manhattan Review*). I'm fascinated by the way we mark and experience time, be it in units of weeks, months, years. This fascination with time goes back as far as my poem 'The World Has Passed', from my first collection *The Orchard Upstairs* (OUP, 1980) where I describe twelve alternative months. The phrase, 'the world has passed' is a Yokut Native American Indian term meaning 'a year has gone by'. I was inspired in the writing of this early poem by Peter Redgrove's poem A 'Twelvemonth', and by U.A. Fanthorpe's 'Words for Months'.

In 'The Year Strikes the Rock' I've looked at the varied personalities of one imaginary year—seeing it as a spoilt child, a goddess, a sleepless person, someone who yearns for solitude, to 'live in/a leaky green caravan in Cadiz/or in an attic some place / where the world won't think of looking for her . . .' The year then takes on the identity of a journeying mapmaker in an Arctic landscape who carves maps in ivory, maps which are at once out of date (for the ice landscape shifts and changes, is not stable)—this implies the remorseless onward drive of time which is always in motion, time never stands still.

Towards the close of the poem I allow myself to experience the transgressive pleasure (for a woman) of having hairy armpits; this body experience is one our current culture does not permit me, or rather, I am not brave enough to flout the norm. But in the realm of imagination I can, and do. In the last couplet time turns back to look at the historic figure of Martin Luther's wife. I hope I communicate here the transformative nature of the year, of event, persona and weather, the magic of renewing sunlight, the sense of wholeness within the bright circle of the wedding ring. Every turning year, serpent with tail in mouth, enables us to mark out a circle of time where we may contain and contemplate and enact our life."

JON STONE was born in Derby and lives in Whitechapel. He is co-creator of micro-anthology publishers Sidekick Books and arts magazine *Fuselit*, as well as various collaborative live events in London. He was highly commended in the National Poetry Competition 2009, the same year his debut pamphlet, *Scarecrows*, was published by Happenstance. A full collection, *School of Forgery*, is due out from Salt in 2012. He also co-edited the anthology *Birdbook I: Towns, Parks, Gardens and Woodland* with Kirsten Irving. He comments, "The form of this poem (every line ends with an anagram of the word 'mustard') is one I'd been wanting to attempt for some time but I had to wait for the right word to occur to me—one that I felt had a certain untapped potential, which initially seemed mundane but could be teased out and made to take on an almost mystic resonance when split apart and put back together in different ways. Like much of what I write, the poem is part tall story, part invocation. Our actions hinge on our beliefs and I tend to think poetry has the power to nudge beliefs in a certain direction, ie that poets deal in carefully controlled fictions that might just have a hint of truth about them. Perhaps if you read this and remember it, the next time you eat mustard from a jar, you'll feel something of the effect described here. The idea of being able to shift the mud around someone's heart and to expunge some of their pain through long distance contact is, I think, one of the main moral purposes of literature."

MATTHEW SWEENEY was born in Donegal in 1952, and is based in Cork currently, having previously been resident in Berlin, Timi oara and, for a long time, London. His latest publication is *The Night Post—A New Selection* (Salt, 2010). Several books prior to that, including *Black Moon*, (2007), Sanctuary (2004) and *Selected Poems* (2002) were all published by Cape. His children's collections, including *Up on the Roof—New and Selected Poems*, have been published by Faber. He is co-author, with John Hartley Williams, of *Writing Poetry* (Hodder), and editor, or co-editor of several anthologies. He writes, "My daughter had a baby girl, my first grandchild. I visited them in Belfast, to see and hold the little one. On my departure, my daughter said she expected a poem to mark the joyous arrival. I objected, saying those poems were the most impossible to write. And anyway, I said, if I could write one, it would be weird. She said weird was good. So I headed off to George Best airport, to fly back to Cork, with my daughter's words and expectation ringing in my ears. I purchased several small bottles of red wine, while waiting for the announcement to board the plane, and started scribbling on a piece of paper. When I got to Cork I had a draft that seemed surprisingly promising. I should add that I'd attempted several poems for my own children (daughter and son) when they were little, and none of those attempts seemed now particularly successful. Somehow the extra distance of a grandchild had, apparently, proved liberating. "

GEORGE SZIRTES was born in Hungary and came to England as a refugee in 1956. His work includes over a dozen volumes of poetry and a roughly equal number of volumes of translation, as well as a miscellaneous collection of other books. He was joint winner of the Faber Memorial Prize with his first book, *The Slant Door* (1979) and the T.S. Eliot Prize for *Reel* (2004), for which he was short-listed again in 2009. His *New and Collected Poems* (2008) was named one of The Independent's Books of the Year. He comments, "After the publication of my *New and Collected Poems* (2008) and the book that had mostly been already written but was designed to follow it, *The Burning of the Books and Other Poems* (2009) I was—and still am—interested in extending the range of my writing, to try voices and forms I hadn't used on themes I hadn't written about. The collaboration with three visual artists—Phyllida Barlow, Caroline Wright and Helen Rousseau—was an ideal opportunity to do so. The work to which the poem is a response, Rousseau's 'Border 0.7' doesn't show a snake—it is a black and white pattern that might perhaps suggest a snake in its banding. The border reminded me of some folk-patterns of the kind I was asked to provide as a small child in my school exercise books in Hungary.

The poem arises from such faint sources but the theme of the snake and the mode of proverbial folk saying were immediately attractive. The process of writing does not, of course, consist of such vague grabs at intention ('I will write about this in such and such a way')—it is improvisatory and compulsive, a partial letting go into the unconscious. The lines as they first appeared came out of such a space, more or less as they are now, though the form of the poem wriggled down the page. The trouble with this was that the wriggling ran the sayings into each other. It felt better to have them as hard and dry statements with line spacing. They carried more authority that way. Its sister poem, 'Snake Ghost' (many of the project poems were written as pairs) did the wriggling instead. But this poem is clearly big sister. Do I believe in the sayings as propositions? I don't know. I don't even know what the question means. I believe in their authority, which is all that matters. Compulsive authority—another term for poetry—does not start out as truth: in its own peculiar and provisional rhythmic way it becomes truth. The poem will appear in my next book, *Bad Machine*."

LIZZI THISTLETHWAYTE is a bookbinder and paper conservator who prefers to make poems.

She lives and works on the Norfolk/Suffolk border. Her poetry has been published in *Smiths Knoll*, *The Rialto*, *Poetry Wales*, *Obsessed With Pipework*, *Modern Poetry in Translation* and *Versal*. Her pamphlet *No Map* was published in 2009. She comments, "Scart Gap was a place on the coast near our home where we used to go with my father, a wild place of marram grass, sand and shingle banks. But when I look for it on a map I can't find it. Maybe it was a gap in the ever shifting sandbanks through which, at high water, a vessel of shallow draught could make safe passage? I don't know. I clearly remember the words Scart Gap. I loved the sound of those words (scart means a gust of wind or a strip of cloud, or a cormorant). I know we went there. Making the poem became an exploration of both the intense visual imagery of my internal landscape and an external landscape that I couldn't quite fathom out but at the same time was utterly familiar with. Two inter-tangled landscapes. There is a lonely note in the poem, but it's also about want, about uncertainty. It is, above all, an exploration, a journey into an uncharted place of huge skies."

EOGHAN WALLS' first collection *The Salt Harvest* is due out with Seren in October, 2011. He won an Eric Gregory Award in 2006, and has published his poetry in a range of journals and anthologies. He completed a PhD in the Seamus Heaney Centre for Poetry at Queen's, Belfast in 2008, and currently teaches for the Open University. He lives on the Irish coast with his wife and two daughters. He comments, "An approach I often take is trying to make the poem contain its own opposite. In this case, that meant wide horizons contrasted against a small body; the end of human life contrasted against the survival of one. The long lines mirrored the horizon of the ocean. I stuck to half-rhymes, and hid them from the eye by splitting the rhymes with a verse-break.

I am suspicious of environmental awareness in poetry — it can be preachy, and lead to the death of a poem. However, back when I wrote this, I considered environmental concerns not as an ethical problem, but rather as a method of re-envisioning the world: an apocalyptic transformation, much akin to the apocalypses offered by Christianity or science fiction. A stark cleansing of the world.

At the same time, I had been teaching our firstborn to walk — or rather, practising her stamping reflex against the bathwater. We'd had a lot of bad news in the year leading up to her birth — a series of deaths and cancers — small apocalypses in themselves. In some ways her birth was an act of defiance. Her movements were laughable, ridiculous even, but had the power to transform us. I hoped to make an imprint of her gangling, messianic power here."

AHREN WARNER was born in 1986. His first collection, *Confer*, is published by Bloodaxe in 2011 and is a PBS Recommendation and shortlisted for the Forward Prize for Best First Collection. He has also published a pocket book, *Re:*, with Donut Press and received an Eric Gregory Award in 2010. He is currently working on a PhD at the University of London. He writes, "*Hasard* is primarily translated from the French as 'chance', though it also contains a related secondary meaning of 'risk' or 'danger'. In the sixth stanza of the poem, the phrase '*lits hasardeux*' refers to Baudelaire's poem *Brumes et pluies* ('Mist and Rain') in which he writes '*Rien n'est plus doux . . . Que l'aspect permanent de vos pâles ténèbres*' ('Nothing is sweeter . . . than the permanence of your pale shadows') referring to his eponymous subject matter. He continues: '*Si ce n'est, par un soir sans lune, deux à deux,/D'endormir la douleur sur un lit hasardeux.*' ('Unless it is a moonless night, side by side/in an accidental bed, the lull of suffering'). 'Hasard' is, partially, a poem about 'beds of chance', about the temporary or permanent beds we find ourselves in. It is also, partially, about the chance paths one takes to such locales. When, in stanza four, the poem's voice states 'You lack the intellect' it is, in some sense, literal. In another sense it is a statement of *le manque* (the 'lack', but also 'want', 'desire' etc.) of the intellect when confronted with these chance routes and the accidental beds they end up in."

CHRISSY WILLIAMS lives in London and has had work in various magazines including *The Rialto, Horizon Review, Anon, Fuselit* and *Rising*. Her work has also appeared in recent anthologies *Stop Sharpening Your Knives 4, Starry Rhymes: 85 Years of Allen Ginsberg* and in several anthologies published by Sidekick Books. She is Joint Editor of *Poetry Digest*, the world's finest edible poetry journal, and has an MA in Modern and Contemporary Poetry. She is the coordinator for the Saison Poetry Library's magazine digitisation project at www.poetrymagazines.org.uk. A pamphlet *Flashes of Light* is forthcoming from Holdfire Press.

She comments, "Sheep don't have a reputation for being high octane as a species. I wanted to give them something to write home about. The final word is meant to contrast the previously passive and largely present continuous sheep. The use of the plural noun was inspired by the twitter account @dogsdoingthings which recounts scenes from films, replacing the protagonists with dogs. It was originally written for an 'Alternative Nativity' poetry event organised by BroadCast in London at Christmas 2010 and was later published by *Rising*. The invocation of the Terminator mythology serves to subvert the traditional nativity by placing salvation in the hands of men, or in this case sheep, rather than deferring responsibility to the unknown. My particular Terminator fetish is my own business, though I suppose a second unofficial dedication is due to Michael Biehn, a constant source of inspiration. Ultimately, I didn't want these sheep to be the sheep of our stereotyping. I wanted them to be the sheep of every sheep's dreaming."

SAMANTHA WYNNE-RHYDDERCH has published two collections, the latest of which, *Not in These Shoes* (Picador, 2008) was shortlisted for Wales Book of the Year 2009. She has received awards for her work from the Society of Authors (2007), the Hawthornden Foundation (2005) and the Welsh Academy (1997 and 2002). Her third collection will be published by Picador in Summer 2012. She comments, "Lining objects up on tables has always fascinated me, whether pens, pencils, paper, cutlery or tools: the angle of implements creates its own language. By virtue of their place on the table, the tools of eating, writing or building somehow speak for themselves. Transferring this fascination from the table to the page, to write a poem in which I could connect cutlery and communication took some time. It was only when I attended a table etiquette course in Somerset three years ago that I was able to begin writing the poem. After that, the poem came together very quickly, largely because it had already been fermenting in my subconscious for so long before I distilled it onto the page."

MICHAEL ZAND was born in Iran but has spent most of his life in London. He lives near Reading and is a research student and visiting lecturer at Roehampton University. He has participated in various collaborations with musicians and sound artists and recently completed a narrative piece, 'lion', which is available from Shearsman Books. Other projects include the blogsite proetics and a ongoing international translation project called lexico, for which he won the Roehampton Poetry Performance Prize in 2008. He is working on a contemporary translation of *The Rubaiyat of Omar Khayyam* entitled *The Ruby Murray of Omer Kayyam*. He comments, "I wrote 'on a persian cairn' for the *Freak Lung* reading at the Morden Tower, Newcastle, in July 2010. Basil Bunting was a regular at this iconic venue in the 1960s and 70s, but in his earlier years he had lived and worked in Iran. This poem is a kind of imagined dialogue between Bunting and the Persian Modernist poet Forough Farrokhzad. The piece borrows heavily from both of their work, but mashes these references together to create something new and perhaps unexpected. The 'cairn' of the title refers to Farrokhzad's gravestone at Zahir-o-dowleh cemetery in Tehran. In his poem 'Briggflatts', Bunting refers to a stonemason tapping marble 'to a lark's twitter'—I am particularly interested in the notion that this stonemason might be chiselling something in Persian, perhaps a message for Forough. I explore in this poem the possibility that in some spiritual sense these chiselled words might fly across the page, to another part of the world, to Forough's graveside."

LIST OF MAGAZINES

Agenda, The Wheelwrights,
Fletching Street, Mayfield
East Sussex TN20 6TL
Editor: Patricia McCarthy

Ambit, 17 Priory Gardens
London N6 5QY
Editor: Martin Bax

Brittle Star, PO Box 56108,
London E17 0AY
Editors: Louisa Hooper,
Jacqueline Gabbitas, David Floyd,
Martin Parker

The Dark Horse, 3A Blantyre
Mill Road, Bothwell, South
Lanarkshire, G71 8DD
Editor: Gerry Cambridge

Edinburgh Review, 22a Buccleuch
Place, Edinburgh EH8 9LN

Envoi, Meirion House, Glan
yr afon Tanygrisiau, Blaenau
Ffestiniog, Gwynedd, LL41 3SU
Editor: Jan Fortune Wood

Equinox, Chemin de Cambieure
11240 Cailau, Aude, France
Editor: Barbara Dordi

Fuselit, www.fuselit.co.uk/
Editors: Kirsten Irving, Jon Stone

Gutter Magazine,
www.guttermag.co.uk/
Editors: Adrian Searle, Colin Begg

Horizon Review,
www.saltpublishing.com/horizon/
Editor: Katy Evans-Bush

Ink Sweat and Tears,
www.ink-sweat-and-tears.com/
Editor: Helen Ivory

Iota, PO Box 7721, Matlock
DE4 9DD
Editor: Nigel McLoughlin

The London Magazine, 11 Queen's
Gate, London SW7 5EL
Editor: Steven O'Brien

Magma, 23 Pine Walk,
Carshalton SM5 4ES

Mslexia Publications Limited
PO Box 656,
Newcastle upon Tyne, NE99 1PZ
Editor: Debbie Taylor

nineerrors Freak Lung,
www.ninerrors.blogspot.com/
Editor: Linus Slug

Northwords Now, PO Box 15066
Dunblane FK15 5BP
Editor: Chris Powici

Obsessed with Pipework, 8 Abbot's
Way, Pilton, Somerset BA4 4BN
Editor: Charles Johnson

Other Poetry, Fourlawshill
Top, Bellingham, Hexham,
Northumberland, NE48 2EY
Editors: Peter Armstrong, Peter
Bennet, James Roderick Burns,
Crista Ermiya

PN Review, Dept. of English,
University of Glasgow, 5
University Gardens, Glasgow,
G12 8QH
Editor: Michael Schmidt

Poetry London, 81 Lambeth Walk,
London SE11 6DX
Editor: Colette Bryce

Poetry Review, The Poetry Society,
22 Betterton Street, London,
WC2H 9BX
Editor: Fiona Sampson

Poetry Wales, 57 Nolton Street,
Bridgend, Wales, CF31 3AE UK
Editor: Zoë Skoulding

QUID
www.barquepress.com/quid.html
Editor: Andrea Brady

The Rialto, PO Box 309,
Aylesham, Norwich NR11 6LN
Editor: Michael Mackmin

Rising, 80 Cazenove Road, Stoke
Newington, London, N16 6AA
Editor: Tim Wells

Shadowtrain,
www.shadowtrain.com/
Editor: Ian Seed

Shearsman, 58 Velwell Road,
Exeter, EX4 4LD
Editor: Tony Frazer

Smiths Knoll, Goldings, Goldings
Lane, Leiston, Suffolk, IP16 4EB
Editors: Michael Laskey and
Joanna Cutts

South Bank Poetry, 74 Sylvan
Road, London, SE19 2RZ
Editor: Peter Ebsworth

Staple, 114–116 St. Stephen's
Road, Sneinton, Nottingham,
NG 2 4JS
Editor: Wayne Burrows

Stop Sharpening Your Knives,
www.stopsharpeningyourknives.
co.uk/
Editors: Emily Berry, Nathan
Hamilton, Sam Riviere and Jack
Underwood

Tears in the Fence, 38 Hod View,
Stourpaine, Blandford Forum,
Dorset, DT11 8TN
Editor: David Caddy

Wasafiri, The Open University in
London, 1–11 Hawley Crescent,
Camden Town, London,
NW1 8NP
Editor: Susheila Nasta

The Warwick Review, Department
of English, University of Warwick
Coventry CV4 7AL
Editor Michael Hulse

New Welsh Review, PO Box 170, Aberystwyth, Ceredigion, SY23 1WZ
Editor: Gwen Davies

The Wolf, April Heights, Fagnal Lane, Winchmore Hill, Amersham HP7 0PG
Editor: James Byrne

ACKNOWLEDGEMENTS

Grateful acknowledgement is made to the publications from which the poems in this volume were chosen. Unless specifically noted otherwise, copyright to the poems is held by the individual poets.

Gillian Allnutt: "in her kitchen" appeared in *Poetry Review*. Reprinted by permission of the poet.

Mike Bannister: "Satin Moth" appeared in *Other Poetry*. Reprinted by permission of the poet.

Chris Beckett: "Boast of the Fly-Whisk" appeared in *Smiths Knoll*. Reprinted by permission of the poet.

Emily Berry: "Sweet Arlene" appeared in *Poetry London*. Reprinted by permission of the poet.

Liz Berry: "The Year We Married Birds" appeared in *Brittle Star*. Reprinted by permission of the poet.

Nina Boyd: "Lanterns" appeared in *Iota*. Reprinted by permission of the poet.

James Brookes: "Opiates: Kaliningrad" appeared in *The Wolf*. Reprinted by permission of the poet.

Judy Brown: "The Helicopter Visions" appeared in *Ambit*. Reprinted by permission of the poet.

Mark Burnhope: "Twelve Steps Towards Better Despair" appeared in *Magma*. Reprinted by permission of the poet.

Kayo Chingonyi: "Andrew's Corner" appeared in *Wasafiri*. Reprinted by permission of the poet.

Jane Commane: "Music" appeared in *Tears in the Fence*. Reprinted by permission of the poet.

Fred D'Aguiar: "The Rose of Toulouse" appeared in *Poetry London*. Reprinted by permission of the poet.

Emma Danes: "17" appeared in *Poetry News*. Reprinted by permission of the poet.

Amy De'Ath: "Lena at the Beach" appeared in *QUID*. Reprinted by permission of the poet.

Isobel Dixon: "A Beautifully Constructed Cocktail" appeared in *Magma*. Reprinted by permission of the poet.

Sasha Dugdale: "Shepherds" appeared in *Agenda*. Reprinted by permission of the poet.

Ian Duhig: "Jericho Shandy" from *Pandorama* (Picador, 2010). Copyright © Ian Duhig. Originally appeared in *Poetry Review*. Reprinted by permission of Picador.

Josh Ekroy: "78 rpm" appeared in *Equinox*. Reprinted by permission of the poet.

Laura Elliott: "White Lace Nightgown" appeared in *Iota*. Reprinted by permission of the poet.

Carrie Etter: "Prairie" from *Divining for Starters* (Shearsman, 2011). Copyright © Carrie Etter. Originally appeared in *Shearsman*. Reprinted by permission of Shearsman Books.

Dai George: "Poolside at Le Domaine" appeared in *Poetry Wales*. Reprinted by permission of the poet.

Giles Goodland: "Waves" appeared in *Shadowtrain*. Reprinted by permission of the poet.

Matthew Gregory: "Young Pterodactyl" appeared in *Stop Sharpening Your Knives*. Reprinted by permission of the poet.

Philip Gross: "Later" appeared in *Poetry London*. Reprinted by permission of the poet.

Kelly Grovier: "A Butterfly in the British Museum" appeared in *PN Review*. Reprinted by permission of the poet.

Jen Hadfield: "The Ambition" appeared in *Magma*. Reprinted by permission of the poet.

Aiko Harman: "Hitodama (人魂 or 'Human Soul')" appeared in *Edinburgh Review*. Reprinted by permission of the poet.

Emily Hasler: "Valediction" appeared in *The Rialto*. Reprinted by permission of the poet.

Oli Hazzard: "Sonnet" appeared in *PN Review*. Reprinted by permission of the poet.

W.N. Herbert: from "Errant" appeared in *The Warwick Review*. Reprinted by permission of the poet.

Alexander Hutchison: "Deil Tak The Hinmaist" appeared in *Gutter*. Reprinted by permission of the poet.

Sarah Jackson: "Light Over Ratcliffe" appeared in *Staple*. Reprinted by permission of the poet.

Christopher James: "The Retired Eunuch" appeared in *Iota*. Reprinted by permission of the poet.

Katharine Kilalea: "Hennecker's Ditch" appeared in *PN Review*. Reprinted by permission of the poet.

Nick Laird: "Collusion" appeared in *Poetry London*. Reprinted by permission of the poet.

Pippa Little: "Coal End Hill Farm 1962" appeared in *Northwords Now*. Reprinted by permission of the poet.

Chris McCabe: "Kingfisher" appeared in *The Rialto*. Reprinted by permission of the poet.

Ted McCarthy: "Beverly Downs" appeared in *Envoi*. Reprinted by permission of the poet.

John McCullough: "Sleeping Hermaphrodite" appeared in *Poetry London*. Reprinted by permission of the poet.

Patrick McGuinness: "House Clearance" from *Jilted City* (Carcanet, 2010) appeared in *Agenda*. Reprinted by permission of Carcanet Press.

Kona Macphee: "My Life as a B Movie" appeared in *Poetry London*. Reprinted by permission of the poet.

Lorraine Mariner: "And then there will be no more nonsense" appeared in *The Rialto*. Reprinted by permission of the poet.

Sophie Mayer: "Of Other Spaces (Tate St. Ives)" appeared in *Agenda*. Reprinted by permission of the poet.

Gordon Meade: "Rats" appeared in *Gutter*. Reprinted by permission of the poet.

Matt Merritt: "Pluvialis" from *hydrodaktulopsychicharmonica* (Nine Arches, 2010). Copyright © Matt Merritt. Originally appeared in *Iota*. Reprinted by permission of Nine Arches Press.

Kate Miller: "The Apple Farmers' Calendar" appeared in *New Welsh Review*. Reprinted by permission of the poet.

Esther Morgan: "Short-hold" appeared in *Mslexia*. Reprinted by permission of the poet.

Catherine Ormell: "Delicacy" appeared in *Smiths Knoll*. Reprinted by permission of the poet.

Richard Osmond: "Logo" appeared in *Fuselit*. Reprinted by permission of the poet.

Ruth Padel: "Only Here On Earth" appeared in *New Welsh Review*. Reprinted by permission of the poet.

Emma Page: "California" appeared in *Poetry London*. Reprinted by permission of the poet.

Nii Ayikwei Parkes: "Lapse" from *The Makings of You* (Peepal Tree, 2010). Copyright © Nii Ayikwei Parkes. Originally appeared in *South Bank Poetry*. Reprinted by permission of the poet.

Abigail Parry: "Hare" appeared in *The Rialto*. Reprinted by permission of the poet.

Andrew Philip: "10 X 10" appeared in *Gutter*. Reprinted by permission of the poet.

Heather Phillipson: "At First, the Only Concern is Milk, More or Less" appeared in *The Rialto*. Reprinted by permission of the poet.

Kate Potts: "Three Wishes" appeared in *The Wolf*. Reprinted by permission of the poet.

Vidyan Ravinthiran: "Anti-circ" appeared in *Horizon Review*. Reprinted by permission of the poet.

Deryn Rees-Jones: from "The Songs of Elisabeth So" appeared in *Poetry London*. Reprinted by permission of the poet.

Sam Riviere: "Honeymoon" appeared in *Ambit*. Reprinted by permission of the poet.

Colette Sensier: "Orpheus" appeared in *Iota*. Reprinted by permission of the poet.

Penelope Shuttle: "The Year Strikes the Rock" appeared in *Ink Sweat and Tears*. Reprinted by permission of the poet.

Jon Stone: "Mustard" appeared in *Magma*. Reprinted by permission of the poet.

Matthew Sweeney: "Communiqué" appeared in *The Dark Horse*. Reprinted by permission of the poet.

George Szirtes: "Some Sayings about the Snake" appeared in *Ambit*. Reprinted by permission of the poet.

Lizzi Thistlethwayte: "Scart Gap" appeared in *Obsessed with Pipework*. Reprinted by permission of the poet.

Eoghan Walls: "The Long Horizon" appeared in *The London Magazine*. Reprinted by permission of the poet.

Ahren Warner: "Hasard" appeared in *Magma*. Reprinted by permission of the poet.

Chrissy Williams: "Sheep" appeared in *Rising*. Reprinted by permission of the poet.

Samantha Wynne-Rhydderch: "Table Manners" appeared in *New Welsh Review*. Reprinted by permission of the poet.

Michael Zand: "on a persian cairn" appeared in *nineerrors Freak Lung*. Reprinted by permission of the poet. Reprinted by permission of the poet.